"Chuck and Jenni have hearts for Christ and hearts for kids. Both are found within these pages."

MAX LUCADO, BESTSELLING AUTHOR AND SENIOR MINISTER, OAK HILLS CHURCH OF CHRIST, SAN ANTONIO, TEXAS

"Chuck and Jenni are the real deal...and they have *awesome* kids. But don't worry, this isn't a "Barbie and Ken Guide to Perfect Parenting"—this is a book to encourage real moms and dads dealing with real life problems. Chuck and Jenni emphasize *progress,* not *perfection.* So relax, read, laugh, and be inspired to enjoy your kids, without sacrificing your marriage or your sanity."

BECKY FREEMAN, NATIONAL SPEAKER AND BESTSELLING AUTHOR OF *WORMS IN MY TEA* AND *LIFE NOTES: A SURVIVAL GUIDE FOR PARENTS OF PRESCHOOLERS*

"Chuck and Jenni Borsellino have hit a home run! With hilarious real-life stories, practical parenting principles, and hands-on advice based on biblical truth, their new book will capture your heart from the first paragraph through the final chapter. *How to Raise Totally Awesome Kids* is fast-paced, upbeat, fun, and down-to-earth. If you are raising a kid, or if you just *know* a kid, this book is for you!"

CAROL KENT, ACCLAIMED AUTHOR, SPEAKER, AND PRESIDENT OF SPEAK UP SPEAKER SERVICES

"Great people write great books and raise great kids. I know Chuck and Jenni well, and they're as good offscreen as they are on. You'll love their book! It's practical and entertaining. You'll walk away with the determination that you can make this wonderful journey of raising kids."

DR. KEVIN LEMAN, AUTHOR OF *MAKING CHILDREN MIND WITHOUT LOSING YOURS* AND HOST OF THE TELEVISION SHOW *REALFAMILIES.COM*

"*How to Raise Totally Awesome Kids* is the quintessential Chuck and Jenni—funny, honest, encouraging, and *real*. Their ring-true stories and gentle, wise advice demonstrate not only how to be a better parent, but also what to do when we fall down on the job. As a wife and mother of two teens, I connected with every example, found myself laughing and crying all the way through, and finished the book determined to make parenting my highest priority."

LIZ CURTIS HIGGS, AUTHOR OF *MIXED SIGNALS* AND *BOOKENDS*

"The surprising benefit and secret power of Chuck and Jenni's wonderful *How to Raise Totally Awesome Kids* is that it also teaches the *parent* how to become a totally awesome *person*. 'You can't teach what you don't know, and you can't pass on what you don't have,' they write. With honesty and humor, they share their own family stories, invaluable insights, and practical tools to help you become an authentic, principle-centered parent whose kids will gladly follow in your footsteps."

NANCY STAFFORD, AUTHOR OF *BEAUTY BY THE BOOK*

HOW TO RAISE
TOTALLY AWESOME
KIDS

Dr. Chuck & Jenni
Borsellino

Multnomah®Publishers *Sisters, Oregon*

HOW TO RAISE TOTALLY AWESOME KIDS
published by Multnomah Publishers, Inc.

Published in association with the literary agency of
Alive Communications, Inc.
7680 Goddard Street, Suite 200, Colorado Springs, CO 80920

© 2002 by Chuck and Jenni Borsellino

International Standard Book Number: 1-57673-881-7

Cover design by Kirk DouPonce/UDG DesignWorks
Cover image by Image Bank

Unless otherwise indicated, Scripture quotations are from:
The Holy Bible, New King James Version © 1984 by Thomas Nelson, Inc.

Other Scripture quotations:
The Holy Bible, New International Version (NIV) © 1973, 1984 by International
Bible Society, used by permission of
Zondervan Publishing House

The Holy Bible, King James Version (KJV)

Holy Bible, New Living Translation (NLT) © 1996. Used by permission of
Tyndale House Publishers, Inc. All rights reserved.

Multnomah is a trademark of Multnomah Publishers, Inc.,
and is registered in the U.S. Patent and Trademark Office.
The colophon is a trademark of Multnomah Publishers, Inc.

Printed in the United States of America

For information:
MULTNOMAH PUBLISHERS, INC.
POST OFFICE BOX 1720
SISTERS, OREGON 97759

Library of Congress Cataloging-in-Publication Data
Borsellino, Chuck.
  How to raise totally awesome kids / by Chuck and Jenni Borsellino.
    p. cm.
Includes bibliographical references.
    ISBN 1-57673-881-7
  1. Child rearing--Religious aspects--Christianity. I. Borsellino, Jenni. II. Title.
  BV4529 .B67 2002
  248.8'45--dc21   2002005810

02 03 04 05 06 07 08—10 9 8 7 6 5 4 3 2 1 0

Dedication

It is with great pride and greater pleasure
that we dedicate this book to those who have taught us most
about the process of living, loving, and learning:

Our Savior...
who has taught us how to live abundantly.

Our parents...
who have taught us how to learn continually.

Our kids...
who have taught us how to love enthusiastically!

CONTENTS

ACKNOWLEDGMENTS

A HEARTFELT THANK-YOU to those who made these pages possible....

To FamilyNet, who allows us the privilege to live out our dream on the *At Home—Live! with Chuck & Jenni* program. You offer us the opportunity to model the message of faith, family, and friendship each day. The production team turns noise into music. The management team keeps the band on Broadway!

To Multnomah Publishers, who encouraged us, inspired us...and set deadlines that almost killed us! This relationship has all the ingredients for a long and happy marriage. We're blessed to hold hands with you. You feel like family.

To our editors, Renee DeLoriea and Jennifer Gott, whose keen eyes and sharp minds saw that some chapters needed watering while others needed a weed whacker! We gave you a gallon of paint, and you turned it into a work of art.

To Chip MacGregor, a promoter, a protector, and a partner who comes disguised as a literary agent. You are the wind that makes our kite soar.

To Julie O'Brien, who offered her pen, her paper, and her pageantry to make our memories come alive. You offered us a cup of cold water for a dry and parched mind. Never underestimate your calling or your competence.

To Bob, Shane, and Jeff, who prayed for us when our backs were against the wall. You provided for us when our

9

pockets were empty. You carried us when our knees were weak and our burdens were heavy. May God grant us the opportunity to do the same for you one day.

To our kids, Brittany, Cody, and Courtney, who took the time from their busy schedules to train two newborn parents. You have transformed our life from black-and-white to Technicolor. Every parent should be so fortunate to be raised by kids like you.

To our Savior, whose promises are true and whose principles are trustworthy. You bring great peace to our hearts and great promise to our hereafter. This is Your work. Thank You for loving us, leading us…and never letting go of us.

To the reader, we thought of you every hour. We prayed for you every day. We trust that this resource will provide peace for your heart and provision for your home. We're honored that you would invite us to come home with you.

The Power of Principle-Centered Parenting

Parents are the last people on earth who ought to have children.

Samuel Butler

IT'S EVERY MOTHER'S NIGHTMARE. The phone call every parent dreads.

"Hello, Mrs. Borsellino. My name is Mr. Leggett, and I'm the principal at Caldwell Elementary School. Are you Cody's mom?"

My standard response is, "That depends."

Instantly I realize that this can't be good. Principals don't call to let us know that our kids are a delight to have in class and to ask if we may have more hidden around our house somewhere.

No, principals do the hard work. Principals make the tough calls. Principals deal with the tough kids—the testy, the taxing, and the troublesome.

The conversation continues. "I just thought you'd want to know that during recess today Cody got into the teachers' supply cabinet, found some finger paints, and repainted rooms 2A and 2B, the library, the teachers' lounge, and a substitute teacher a bright shade of persimmon orange."

My jaw hits the floor. My blood pressure hits the ceiling.

"Mrs. Borsellino, it's not that we want to stifle Cody's creativity or wound his sensitive self-esteem, but the consensus among the teachers, staff, counselors, custodians, and lawn care personnel here at Caldwell is that disciplinary action is in order. Um, Mrs. Borsellino? Mrs. Borsellino…are you still there?"

When I come to, I think to myself, *Good parents just don't have days like this, do they?*

I thank the principal and hang up the phone.

Then my mind races to a dozen questions about:

- the personal—what kind of mom am I?
- the principal—what does he think of me?
- the parental—where did we go wrong?
- the price tag—how much will it cost to fix?

I wonder how I'm going to deal with this situation, but then I find the answer—seven words that have been handed down since recorded history. Just as my mother before me discovered, these seven words will release my burden, relieve my dismay, and reduce my shame: "Just wait till your dad comes home!"

Sound familiar?

I've been there, done that, and have the medication to prove it. (Do the terms Prozac, Paxil, and Zoloft mean anything to you?) But since then, I've discovered that it doesn't have to be this way.

PRINCIPLE-CENTERED PARENTING

Since that infamous day, Chuck and I have discovered ten principles that will change your life, deepen your faith, and transform your family. Not principals like the one sitting behind a golden oak desk at your local school; these principles are internal and lie deep within our character. They provide a compass to help us navigate the "parent map." These principles will help parents deal with the tough calls: the testy, the taxing, and the troublesome challenges of parenting.

These principles are tested and timeless. You can count on them when your parental back is against the wall. They are the kind of principles that will make a difference when your kids are rebelling, your patience is failing, and your blood pressure is rising.

HERE'S THE PLAN

Chuck and I are inviting you to sit with us in a secluded corner of Starbucks—where the coffee's hot, the music's soft, and the challenges we're going to discuss are real. We have our kids on our minds and our hearts on our sleeves.

We've sat here a thousand times, with a thousand parents just like you. We can see the frustration in your eyes: a mom who feels exhausted, a wife who feels discouraged, a woman who feels depleted. Oh yeah, and a dad so frustrated that golf seems like fun!

Don't panic. You've come to the right place. This is a place where we can talk parent to parent. A place where we will uncover solutions to the parenting problems that plague us most.

I want you to know that:

- there is hope,
- there is help,
- there is humor, and
- there is a heavenly Father who loves you deeply...all of which will get you through this!

Hope, help, and humor will transform an exhausted parent into an effective parent. Collectively, they come from a Father who desires to encourage and equip you to become the parent you've always dreamed of becoming.

Sound too good to be true?

Within the pages of this book, you will discover the premise, the promise, and the practice of Principle-Centered Parenting. If you develop and implement the principles we've outlined, you can once again experience the indescribable joy and incredible fulfillment that result from successful parenting, just as the Master designed it to be.

The Premise

Just like most of you, we were absent the day they taught Parenting 101. As a result, we jumped into parenthood unschooled and unprepared. As a matter of fact, our baby-sitter used to offer us a 20 percent discount for returning home early!

By the end of a typical day, most of our mental, physical, and emotional resources were weathered by our world or consumed by our work. As our kids arrived home, Jenni would stand weary and glassy-eyed, longing for a parental happy hour. Not the pandemonium of a smoked-filled bar, but sixty minutes of peace and tranquillity at home, in bed...*alone!*

Two hours later, I would arrive home. Theory has it that my homecoming would even the odds and lighten the load. So much for theory. In actuality, by this time of day Jenni felt discouraged and I felt deficient!

Like most parents, we had to navigate this journey on our own. An abundance of scholars and schoolbooks were out there, but as we navigated the parent trip, somehow the destination was fuzzy, the signs along the side of the road were dimly lit, and our speed was hopelessly erratic. The map was covered with coffee stains and was crunched under the seat somewhere. And while we were looking for the parent map, we fell into the parent trap. Thank God, our spiritual compass pointed heavenward, so we bent our knees, closed our eyes, and clasped our hands.

Maybe God would help.
He did.

There we were, parents caught in the crossfire between our spiritual convictions and our secular culture. There we were, parents with misguided principles and mistaken priorities.

But we weren't alone.

Before we discovered these principles, we were on a hunt just like many other parents for Barbie dolls and baseball gloves, for cashmere sweaters and custom skateboards. Take a look around. Parenting has focused on purchasing a handful of happiness for our kids. After all, isn't "happiness" what we want for our kids? And that's exactly what most of us attempt to gift-wrap each Christmas, birthday, and special occasion.

According to a study conducted by the Joseph Rowntree Foundation, the average parent spends $385 per child each Christmas and an additional $193 each birthday.[1] "Passing the buck" has taken on a new meaning for parents in the twenty-first century, and unfortunately, most of what we offer our kids has a very short shelf life!

In a recent study designed to identify parental priorities, parents around the world were asked what they desired most for their children. While most Europeans chose "good health" and most Japanese parents desired "success" for their kids, the majority of American parents proudly declared, "We just want our kids to be happy."[2] After all, the pursuit of happiness is guaranteed by the Declaration of Independence! Other nations were formed on pride, power, religion, or roots, but America was founded on the pursuit of happiness.

It's unfortunate, but in our desire to provide happiness as an emotional springboard, many well-intentioned parents have paved the road for their children to live a life of convenience... at the expense of their character.

Instead of focusing on developing children of character, conviction, and courage, we have focused on making our kids happy. Unfortunately, happiness and growth are often at opposite ends of the continuum, and if we choose one, we sacrifice the other. In this land, it's not hard to see the seeds we've planted or predict the fruit we're about to inherit!

Now don't get us wrong, happiness isn't a bad goal; it's just not a great one. When our kids' happiness becomes the hallmark of successful parenthood, our families, our faith, and our foundation are in trouble. Instead, we would like to suggest that effective parents become principle-centered parents and focus more on developing their children's character—and less on their children's comfort.

THE PURPOSE OF A PRINCIPLE

So what holds a family together in a world that is pulling us apart? Principles. Principles to anchor to your conscience. Principles to secure to your soul.

We have discovered ten principles that form the core of what we call principle-centered parenting. We gathered these principles on the road—and on the run. We've gleaned some from the successful and some from the sorrowful. They are the by-product of hundreds of interviews with guests, authors, experts, and entertainers as we hosted the nationally syndicated programs *100 Huntley Street, OpenHouse,* and *At Home—Live! with Chuck & Jenni.* The insights from these people have been tried and tested in our home and have become a parent map that helped us avoid the long and winding road that leads to the parent trap.

Now don't get us wrong—we're far from perfect. There are times when we struggle just like you. The road to parental success runs uphill, so don't expect to break any speed records. Some time ago we discovered that we would succeed as parents not because we were destined to but because we were *determined* to. That determination is what will make the difference between raising average kids and raising *awesome* kids.

If at first you don't succeed...
you're probably just like the rest of us!

Chuck's insight comes from the textbook; mine comes from the trenches. As a psychologist with more than twenty years of clinical practice, Chuck has read it all, heard it all, and counseled it all. As a mom with three kids and fifteen years of "clinical parenting," I've seen it all, done it all, and most importantly, given it my all-in-all. Together, what we have to offer is the best of both worlds: parenting from the textbook and parenting from the trenches—a marriage partnership of education and experience.

But here's the catch: Both of us agree that most lessons learned in the classroom of our homes are caught and not taught. Despite the speeches given at the supper table and the sermons taught from Scripture, our actions speak louder than our intentions, and our conduct speaks louder than our curriculum. We must develop principle-centered lives before we can be principle-centered parents. Our kids will follow our footsteps faster than they will follow our words.

Therefore, the ten principles we propose should be digested before they are dispensed. Why? Because it's impossible to teach something we don't know, to give away something we don't have, or to ask our kids to become someone they've never seen. That's why we believe that:

Well done is better than well said.

George Washington

The Promise

I know what you're thinking:

- easy to endeavor,
- exhausting to achieve,
- impossible to execute.

Unfortunately, parenting offers no recess and no reprieve. That's the bad news. So here's the good news: Principle-centered parenting is designed not only to give you ten ideas for effective and successful parenting, but also to increase the time, energy, and resources you will have available at the end of the day. Time to spend at a candlelit dining table with your spouse, time with a cup of hot coffee and a good book, or time at the mall!

Just imagine, the most difficult decision you might have to make at this time next year could be deciding what to do with your free time!

Imagine life without trips to see the pastor, the principal, the psychologist, or the police. Imagine life with fewer scuffles in the school yard and no bloodshed in the backyard. Imagine life with only rare confrontations between parents and offspring. Too good to be true? Not so.

PRINCIPLE-CENTERED PARENTING MAKES IT POSSIBLE

We're not saying it's going to be easy. Charting a course correction never is. But we're convinced that success hinges on these ten principles. If we learn them, we can live them. If we live them, we can impart them. And if we impart them, then one year from now, with these principles, we will be different parents...

- raising different kids,
- parenting in a different family,
- heading toward a different destination.

Principle-centered parenting will empower you to take

your family to a destination of unlimited potential and unrestricted possibilities. So pack your bags and start the car. Together—joining you as counselor and coach—we're only ten principles away from transforming good parents into great parents and kids of comfort into kids of character.

Oh, by the way, Cody's principal just called, and he doesn't know what to do with his extra time either!

Principle-centered parents:

- live principle-centered lives.
- teach principles from the inside out.
- don't just do things differently, but do different things.
- turn beliefs into behaviors and principles into practice.

The strength of a nation lies in the homes of its people.

ABRAHAM LINCOLN

Chapter One

WHEN ENOUGH
IS NOT ENOUGH...AND
MORE IS NOT AN OPTION

Major on Progress. Minor on Perfection.

*Did this feeling of inadequacy come on suddenly or
did it develop normally with marriage and parenthood?*

UNKNOWN

No one can make you feel inferior without your consent.

ELEANOR ROOSEVELT

LET'S TALK WITH JENNI

EVER WANTED A SECOND CHANCE? Another try? A "do-over"?

In golf, they call it a "mulligan." It's an unofficial shot
that's used regularly by amateur golfers. With a mulligan, if
your ball finds its resting place in the rough, you simply tee up
another ball, adjust for the error, and pretend you never hit the
first one. No wonder people love this game!

What about you?

Ever wish you had a mulligan for every mistake, a do-over for every disappointment, a second chance for every parental faux pas? Wouldn't it be great if parenting came with a mulligan? You know, a child you could practice on before you were ready to tee up your real kids…like a spare pot roast to practice on while another (baked to perfection) waited on the sidelines to replace the practice one? Well, wouldn't it be nice?

I Am Woman, Hear Me Whimper

For me, the idea of having a practice run sounds perfect and was particularly appealing the time my mother arrived…for inspection! She was coming to visit our family. Her flight was on time, her outfit was to die for, and her luggage showed up *with* the plane—a perfect start to my plans for a perfect visit. My mother lives a thousand miles away, so when she visits, it's not just "Mom dropping over." It's more like having Queen Elizabeth over for high tea.

This was a particularly special time for me because we had just moved, so this was my first chance to show Mom my new home, my new world, and my new Crock-Pot! I wanted everything to be perfect. Perfect home, perfect kids equals perfect wife, perfect life. (She knows Chuck, so he's not part of this equation.)

My mother has never desired or demanded perfection from me—she just wants to *be*. She wants to *be* with her grandchildren, to *be* with her daughter, and yes, even to *be* with her darling son-in-law (for shorter periods of time!). But I had other plans.

This was an opportunity to impress my mother, my mentor, my role model. The house was meticulously prepared for display, the kids looked adorable (Chuck looked like Chuck), and even the dog looked suave ("suave" costs thirty-nine dollars at PetSmart).

By now I was basking in my perfection. *Truly, I am an incredible woman. Single-handedly I birthed, bathed, and burped three adorable children. I have a successful career, a semitrained spouse, and a fully trained dog (or is it the other way around?). Not only am I an incredible housekeeper and gardener, but now, here I am, Martha Stewart in the kitchen.* Then, just as I was asking myself, *Is there anything this woman cannot do...?*

The timer went off!

I reached over to take the pot roast out of the Crock-Pot, but there were problems in paradise. My plans for perfection and my short-lived "Martha Stewart" image began to unravel. I discovered that my precious pot roast looked more like ET than the juicy roast I had anticipated. My horror was further compounded when I poked the blob and it bled.

Just then the kids began to argue about who was going to sit next to their "favorite" grandma. Chairs were being shuffled...place mats were being scrambled. Chaos was unfolding. The phone rang and Chuck bolted from his chair. He accidentally knocked over the dog's food dish, and Kibbles 'n Bits now decorated our kitchen floor. Our dog was so happy that he added some leaps and barks to the excitement for good measure. Out of nowhere the kids decided to be helpful, and before I could say a word, two of them dashed to get a broom and walked through the pile of dog food, crushing it into a million pieces. Now, thoroughly crunched Kibbles 'n Bits were ground into my immaculate floor.

I stood there dazed and dumbfounded as the image of my flawless world unraveled before my eyes.

I was on the verge of tears when I looked up and my eyes met my mother's. I felt comfort rather than criticism. I saw a smile, not a smirk. By the look on her face I could read the thought on her mind: *Now I feel at home.*

LET'S TALK WITH CHUCK: WHEN ENOUGH IS NEVER ENOUGH

This chapter's for you if you've concluded that your best isn't good enough. Never was. Never will be.

Growing up, maybe your siblings were given praise…while you were offered consolation. Your thoughts were considered irrelevant, your feelings were minimized, and your impact seemed negligible.

As a teen you weren't thin enough, tall enough, or toned enough. Others went to the parties…while you went to the library. As an adult, you starved yourself for six months…and gained three pounds. As a parent, you feel unprepared, unskilled, and unworthy.

Maybe your son failed the third grade…again. In soccer, he didn't even touch the ball for the entire first half…of the season. Maybe your daughter fell between the social cracks with her classmates. While the other kids came home from Track and Field Day with ribbons on their chests, your kids came home with defeat on their minds and disappointment in their hearts.

As a parent, you're filled with personal self-doubt and pessimism. You've never measured up. The bar is always higher than your body can leap. The checklist is long; the checkmarks are few. You've always struggled with expectations: your parents', your teachers', your own—not to mention your heavenly Father's. You feel emotionally weak and physically weary.

You know there must be a better way. Then you remember—a mulligan! You wonder if it's possible to call a mulligan. *Would it be possible for me to tee up another spouse, another house, another child, another life…and start over? The perfect life has passed me by, and I'm just too pooped to parent.*

> ## PRINCIPLE #1:
> *Major on Progress. Minor on Perfection.*

If this describes you, then now is the time to remember: Just like you, Jenni and I had visions of becoming perfect parents…and then we had kids. We did our best and raised our kids on the trial-and-error method. Unfortunately, most of it was error! As a result, much of the time we felt like salmon swimming upstream during a drought, polar bears searching for ice in the Sahara.

The worst thing about parenting…is kids.

Whether we were measuring personal or parental performance, our goal was perfection but our grade was less than praiseworthy. Although the distance from where we stood to the Promised Land of Perfection was overwhelming, nothing less than parental perfection was acceptable to us. After all, we are…

Driven by the Demon of Perfection

How did so many of us get this way? For most it began with the "parent tapes"—messages we heard loud and clear and often.

"When are you going to get better grades like your sister Brianna?"

"Why can't you run as fast as Nathan? He's even smaller than you."

"Look how small Nikki is. Why, she's so cute, and she hardly eats a thing."

Grades. Performance. Appearance.

The messages were clear. The voices were loud.

We were told that if we tried harder, studied longer, stayed later, ran faster, jumped higher, and looked prettier, the world would be a better place. A safer place. A place where people would love us and never leave us. Perfection became our minimum standard. We believed that mistakes were only for the mentally unprepared, emotionally unstable, physically undisciplined, or spiritually unworthy. Surely we could do better than that.

But the messages didn't stop.
The comparisons didn't end.

Today, most women are convinced that the average man wants to be married to a woman who acts like Mother Teresa in church, Martha Stewart in the kitchen, and a Playboy bunny in the bedroom. They assume that their kids want a mom who is a cross between the pizza delivery boy and a taxi driver. They conclude that their bosses want them to have the brains of Margaret Thatcher, the business mind of Oprah Winfrey, and the body to package it all in a size-three dress.

> *I know what men really want.*
> *They want a close intimate relationship with someone*
> *who will leave them alone!*
> ELAINE BOOSER

On the other hand, most men are convinced that the average woman wants a man like Billy Graham in church, Bob Vila around the house, and Fabio in the bedroom. They assume that their kids want a dad who is as fun loving as Ronald McDonald and as financially well-off as an ATM machine. And to make things worse, they conclude that their employer expects to find Albert Einstein behind the desk— working for minimum wage!

In most cases the expectations we strive for are imagined, but in some cases they are as real as they are regrettable. One Sunday morning a minister was trying to make a point on perfectionism. He looked upon his congregation and sarcastically asked for anyone who knew of a perfect person to please stand up. After a long pause, one mild-mannered gentleman slowly stood to his feet. The minister was surprised and asked him directly, "Do you really know of a perfect person?"

The hesitant man responded, "Why…yes, sir. I do. His name is Martin and he apparently was my wife's first husband."

In addition to the authentic expectations we feel from others and the imagined ones we develop on our own, in Christian circles many of us are bombarded with messages telling us that our happiness is a by-product of our "holiness." After all, there it is in red and white, "Therefore you shall be perfect, just as your Father in heaven is perfect" (Matthew 5:48). But as our spiritual roots grow deeper, we discover that Jesus was challenging us to be unwavering rather than unstable, permanent rather than perfect.

The Anatomy of a Perfectionistic Parent

The truth is, perfectionists are people pleasers. They are driven for acceptance—their own and others. They set high standards for themselves and subtly impose those standards on others. They work well on their own and are self-disciplined, organized, and driven to excel. Even with several irons in the fire, they seldom ask for help. To them, this would be an admission of inadequacy—the "unpardonable sin" for the uncompromising perfectionist.

Like it or not, the Western world rewards the driven, the detailed, and the college-degreed. However, when it comes to life within the walls of a home dominated by a perfectionistic parent, most children are left feeling inadequate. They conclude that what they do (or even worse, who they are) simply doesn't measure up. Never did. Never will.

Perfectionistic parents do more than take an interest in their kids' activities—they take responsibility for their kids' behaviors and choices. They reward compliance and reinforce performance. Every behavior is examined...and every event becomes a final exam.

Managing the "Martha" in All of Us

Who could blame her? Company was at the door, and dinner was still on the stove. This was no backyard barbecue. It was dinner with the Divine. And while Martha was frantically preparing the food, Mary was feeding her soul at the feet of the Master (see Luke 10:38–42).

Two sisters: One who was frustrated. One who was full.

Mary is one who will meander through life, frequently pausing to smell the roses. Martha will not only pick the roses, but also cut the stems at a forty-five-degree angle and arrange them in a vase with baby's breath and ferns! Martha was so busy being "Martha" that she almost missed the Master. We've all been there.

Most of us have missed a burning bush or two along the way because we were too busy mowing the lawn!

Think back. Back to a day when you felt the most unproductive and unworthy...like yesterday! Was it because you were a Mary, sitting at the feet of the Savior, or a Martha, frustrated because the plan wasn't coming together like the perfectionist in you said it was supposed to?

Now travel back again. This time think back to one of the most memorable times you and your family ever had together. A time when you laughed so hard your stomach ached and your lungs gasped for air. Was it a time of excellence or error? Case closed.

Times when we've messed up, goofed up, or just plain given up are great opportunities for us to experience the importance of laughter, the significance of growth, and the value of grace, which are all made possible by our heavenly Father. God has helped Jenni and me on numerous occasions when our load was heavy, our hearts were broken, and our spirits were hungry. It was times like these when our compass pointed heavenward and we bent our knees, closed our eyes, and clasped our hands. It was then, in times of personal brokenness, that a faultless

Father in heaven whispered to me, "It's not about being perfect; it's all about making progress."

Parents still run fastest on their knees.

It's His grace that allows us to laugh at ourselves and see our imperfections as building blocks instead of roadblocks. Suddenly, we realize that perfection isn't our purpose; progress is. Those days when we can't find our keys…can't find our car…can't even find the parking lot…are okay. Only then are we able to break free of our belief that our worth is measured by our work or that our acceptance is based on our achievements. Only then is it possible to give up our goal of being a perfect person, married to a perfect spouse, raising perfect kids…while still living in a land filled with imperfect people!

When we are at our worst, He is at His best.

JENNI'S TIPS FROM THE TRENCHES… TO TURN THINGS AROUND

I discovered most of these lessons from my Savior—and from my sister. On more than one occasion I found myself calling my sister, who had children several years before I did, for help. She seemed to always understand and have suggestions that would help me muddle through most of the parental problems that popped up.

One day I asked her how she got to be such an expert on parenthood. She replied, "Well, usually by doing things the wrong way years before you did!" Her words reminded me that when it comes to parenthood, most of us will need to experience what *doesn't* work before we realize what *does*. Parenting is all about progress…not perfection.

> *Practice makes imperfect.*
> DR. KEVIN LEMAN

And speaking of progress… That day when my mother visited our home, I must admit that I was just another crackpot using a Crock-Pot. But since then, I've learned an invaluable lesson about using a Crock-Pot: From now on I'm going to plug it in!

1. Recognize and reward character, not performance.

It's not about beauty, it's not about grades, and it's not about trophies. Parents who recognize and reward issues of character (kindness, honesty, perseverance, self-control, etc.) are likely to see their children repeat such behavior. Repeat after me:

> "I am so proud of you for not giving up during the soccer game."
> "I was so happy when you volunteered to help me clean up this morning."
> "I really love the way you help others when you see them struggling."
> "I am so proud of you for returning the money to the cashier."

2. Set realistic expectations.

If everyone were an A student, there wouldn't be any need

for grades. If everyone were expected to win every game, there wouldn't be any need to play. Every child wants to succeed, yet nothing is more frustrating than constant failure. Be careful of constant correction. And because nothing motivates more than success, individualize your expectations of your children and make success inevitable.

3.   Expect mistakes.

Perfection is rare, fleeting, and usually accidental. Expect mistakes. Deal with it! Once you discover this truth, there is freedom in imperfection. But bondage is the reward for the perfectionist. Remember, although most advertisers promise us that there are great payoffs to those who have mastered "perfection" (perfect body, perfect house, perfect clothes, etc.), history tells us that only one among us was perfect and He was crucified.

4.   View mistakes as learning experiences.

The difference between failure and experience is defined by the lessons we learn. Wise people make mistakes, rich people make mistakes, good parents make mistakes—they just make them less often. When you recognize a mistake, ask yourself, "What did this experience teach me?" Mistakes are building blocks, opportunities for growth. With every blunder there is a lesson to be learned. We call it "failing successfully."

5.   Teach excellence, not perfection.

Children should be taught to seek excellence, not perfection. No one is perfect, which is why pencils have erasers and keyboards have a backspace button! If perfection is our goal, failure will be our outcome. While perfection is an ever elusive goal, excellence is achievable. Excellence can be achieved in setting the supper table, vacuuming the family room, or putting clothes away. Parents raising "awesome kids" look for opportunities to say, "Well done."

6. Stress personal achievement, not peer competition.

Preschoolers play. School-age children compete. There's a big difference. Once school begins, everything from paper drives to academic achievement is centered on competition. Now kids are compared to their peers, and they want to see how they're doing relative to those around them.

In the school yard, children are no longer satisfied to simply bounce the ball. Now they're focused on bouncing it higher, longer, and faster than their classmates. Therefore, counteract constant comparisons by helping your children establish individual goals and personal objectives.

7. Avoid comparisons.

Comparisons are inevitable, so parents need to contribute to the solution rather than compound the problem. Because kids will compare their looks, their grades, and their abilities to those around them, parents need to recognize and reinforce individual traits and unique capabilities. Again, this is a great opportunity to acknowledge character-related attributes rather than brains, beauty, or bronze.

8. Demonstrate unconditional love.

Conditional love is expressed when a goal is scored, when a race is won…when the conditions are met. Unconditional love is expressed in spite of the circumstances, regardless of the outcome, and whatever the situation. Unconditional love is unwarranted, undeserved, and unmerited. It is love based on personhood rather than on performance.

By loving our kids unconditionally, we reveal our priorities and reflect our principles to them. It means a trip to Dairy Queen following a 24–3 loss. It means a trip to the trophy store to recognize your child as "Sportsman of the Year." It means a banner on the front door declaring that "Totally Awesome Kids Live Here." Notes in his backpack and confetti in her lunch bag are great ways to underscore your love for them, especially when they may question their love for themselves.

9.   Separate performance from personhood.

It's subtle but significant. Most kids are not able to distinguish the difference between what they do and who they are. There is a big difference. When it comes to discipline, be very specific. Communicate that *what they did* may have been a mistake, but that does not mean that *who they are* is a mistake. After all, we all make mistakes, but if children come to believe that they are mistakes (rather than having made a mistake), the battle's over. Their identity is forged and the self-fulfilling prophecy is hard to combat.

To help teenagers distinguish between what they *did* and who they *are,* you may want to use the following disciplinary approach: "What you did was wrong and unacceptable. You made a mistake. But hear me carefully: That does not mean that *you* are a mistake or that you can't do better. I love you. You are a caring and thoughtful person, but what you did today was irresponsible. Now let's talk about it."

10. Post the "Declaration of Imperfection" and live by it!

The following statement summarizes this chapter and can change your parental effectiveness if you read it, remember it, recite it, and practice it.

Declaration of Imperfection

From this day forward, I, _____, declare myself to be an imperfect parent, living with an imperfect spouse, raising imperfect children. I hereby recognize that as a human being I have made mistakes in the past and will make even more in the future. Although I am not excited about my mistakes, I *am* excited about my growth. I have decided that I will no longer be handcuffed by my fear of the future, nor will I be crippled by remorse for the past. When I make a mistake, I will learn from it, I will grow from it, and I will progress beyond it. I will pick myself up and not put myself down. I have come to realize that my worthiness of love is not tied to my accomplishments. As I become a better parent, I will share my shortcomings with my family so that they may also grow from my mistakes. I have decided that from this day forward, I will no longer be driven by a passion for perfection. Instead, I will be inspired by my preference for progress and my desire for growth.

The closest to perfection a person ever comes
is when he fills out a job application form.
STANLEY J. RANDALL

Chapter Two

WHEN PRIORITIES OVERRIDE PRINCIPLES... AND CONDUCT OUTWEIGHS CURRICULUM

First We Develop. Then We Distribute.

*Children will follow your footsteps faster
than they will follow your words.*

<small>UNKNOWN</small>

*Train up a child in the way he should go,
and go that way yourself!*

LET'S TALK WITH JENNI

I HAVE TO ADMIT IT. I'd be the first to go—voluntarily!

I couldn't survive on a deserted island with sixteen strangers for thirty minutes, let alone thirty days. I would be voted off so fast there wouldn't be time for a commercial break! First of all, I'm what you might call a "high maintenance" woman. I'm *not* leaving home without my blow-dryer, curling iron, or facial steam bath—I don't care how much money they offer me.

Are these people nuts?

The success of reality-TV programming has been phenomenal. It all began with Robin Leach. He would sneak us behind the double doors of a Hollywood mansion and into the lives of the rich and famous. Those were the good old days. In less than a decade, we've somehow gone from caviar dreams to outback nightmares, from the lavish to the lacking. We've traded in watching what some have done *with* a million dollars to what some would do *for* a million dollars.

We must have some kind of strange fascination with peeking into the private lives of others. I bet Chuck could come up with one of his fifty-cent psychological words for it! Now, I must admit that a few weeknights at 8 P.M. I caved in to my curiosity. But come on now, would I really miss my bubble bath in order to find out if Billy Bob would eat a dead rat? Not likely! Would I lose an hour of sleep to find out if Gladys would form an alliance with Hildegard so they could vote off Nathan? Not a chance! I say give me good old-fashioned pretend stories with pretend people doing pretend things! Make me laugh, make me giggle—but, please, don't try to entertain me with reality. I experience enough reality within the four walls of my home each day, thank you very much.

And another thing, have you ever noticed the fact that security cameras are popping up everywhere you go? You can't even go into a department store and blow your nose without a surveillance camera and an emergency SWAT team watching you. I was at the ATM the other day, and while I was waiting for my cash to come out (it's always interesting to see if I get money or a memo—you know the kind!), I noticed that a little piece of broccoli had taken residence between my two front teeth (now don't tell me this has never happened to you). Anyhow, there I was, minding my own business, picking my teeth, when suddenly I realized a camera was staring at my tonsils!

Now I know there must be a logical reason for the camera—you know, security stuff—but I have visions of two guys sitting in a security booth somewhere in Dallas saying, "Hey, isn't that Jenni Borsellino from that television program *At Home—Live?* Look, she's picking her teeth! Can you believe her? She missed a spot. Oh look, she has a cavity on M2—ha, ha, ha!" What a fun job those guys must have. Kind of like *Candid Camera* without Allen Funt.

It was then that I came up with a brilliant idea. Instead of watching sixteen total strangers interact with each other at some deserted location, how about watching a typical Christian family deal with typical problems that take place on a typical day? Now, I'm *not* volunteering for this project, mind you, but it did make me wonder: What if a camera caught your whole day on tape without you knowing about it? Imagine every move was monitored, every word was recorded, and every behavior was taped. That's right! From the time you got up in the morning until the time you tucked your kids in bed at night, your every moment was recorded. What would those tapes reveal? What would they say about you today?

This brings to mind some questions that all parents should be asking themselves. What would these tapes:

- report about our priorities?
- reveal about our principles?
- reflect about our personalities?

What would these tapes disclose about our character when:

- your four-year-old spilled his milk at the breakfast table for the second time?
- unfinished homework was discovered in your eleven-year-old's backpack, again?
- the cashier shortchanged you at the checkout counter, but denied it?
- you discovered that your spouse spent another hundred dollars you don't have?

Now, I know what you're thinking: *That couldn't happen to me.* But in reality, the tapes are recording right now…just ask your kids.

LET'S TALK WITH CHUCK: ALL KIDS ARE HOMESCHOOLED

All day long our words are recorded, the tapes are replayed, and our behaviors are evaluated. In some cases, our kids have come to a conclusion. They've formed an opinion. They've rendered a verdict. In other cases, the jury's still out. But in all cases it is important to remember that all of this took place today within the minds of our children, which reminds us that the most critical lessons in life are caught, not taught.

Without a lesson plan to rely on or an education degree to refer to, you've been teaching school today. All day, every day. There is no recess, no spring break, and no summer vacation. Every waking hour, every day, and everywhere you go with your kids, school's in session and they're taking notes.

The exam will take place when their backs are against the wall, when they have to choose between the right way and the easy way—between what they saw and what they were taught. Their "grade" is hanging in the balance, so we must ask ourselves this question: In their moment of decision, will our children recall our conduct or our curriculum?

Before we tell our children about:

- the value of conviction over compromise,
- the benefits of principle-centered living,
- the rewards of relationship with God, or
- the significance of family,

we must first consider the example we have been setting for them:

- at the breakfast table,
- on the phone,
- at the supermarket,
- at the gas station,
- at McDonald's,
- during the soccer game,
- at bedtime.

With this in mind, the importance of our words matching our ways becomes critical and forms the basis for:

Principle #2:
First We Develop. Then We Distribute.

We can't teach what we don't know. We can't give away what we don't have. We can't distribute what we haven't digested.

Just ask Lot.

We don't have to follow in his footsteps. No, it doesn't have to be that way. In fact, if we learn an important principle from this biblical character, we will increase the likelihood that our students will pass the course…because their teachers have done their homework.

But we have to admit that we have…

A Lot to Learn

Crack open the cover of your Bible to the Old Testament. We need to go back, way back.

The story begins in Genesis when a favored family becomes a flawed family. The sins of a husband take root deep within his wife's heart. Then, the flaws of a father are lived out in his children's conduct. This is not a pretty sight.

Just twelve chapters after the peaceful tranquillity of the Garden, Abram and Lot stood at a crossroads, and they agreed that they just couldn't get along. They needed to separate, to go their own ways. Abram took the high road and allowed Lot to choose his homeland: "If you take the left, then I will go to the right; or, if you go to the right, then I will go to the left" (Genesis 13:9). Abram's choice was driven by principle. Lot's choice was driven by desire.

Lot chose the plain of Jordan—the land of plenty, the land that ensured prosperity and pleasure for his family (see Genesis 13:10–11). But he should have known that the shortest distance to wherever you want to go is usually under construction. In Lot's case, it turned out to be the road to moral bankruptcy.

On the other hand, Abram, who knew that principle is more important than possessions, was left to reside in Canaan (see v. 12). God would take care of him. He would do fine because he had chosen principle over possessions.

Lot's plan for prosperity led him to pitch his tent on the outskirts of Sodom. For him, the choice was made—it was character for cash, righteousness for riches. Little did he know this move was about to cost him his possessions…and eventually affect his posterity.

Soon the sin in the city of Sodom was too much for God to overlook (see Genesis 18:20–21). While God saw fit to spare his life, Lot's trophies were buried deep within this town. God had mercy and sent angels to lead Lot's family to safety (Genesis 19:16); but even though they had escaped, Sodom still lived deep within his wife's heart. The pleasures of Sodom still permeated her spirit. As she looked back with desire, her passion led to her penalty. There was no hope for her. Her body became as her spirit: a lifeless pillar of salt (see Genesis 19:26).

Now I must admit that when I first heard this story, I couldn't help but think that Lot's wife was a few bricks shy of a load. What was she thinking? It was clear as crystal, fresh from the dishwasher: "Look ahead and you triumph; look back and you're toast." How hard was that? But then I remembered how many times in my own life God had made it clear to me what

I was to do, where I was to go, and how I was to get there. And I looked back.

I looked to the left. I looked to the right. I looked everywhere—except up—trying to find an alternative. Hoping this was a multiple-choice offer, I hunted for a better option.

> I don't have time for devotions now; I'll do it later.
>
> We don't have the money to tithe now; we'll give when we do.
>
> My neighbor won't like the pastor; I'll invite her to church when he leaves.
>
> I don't know what to say to her in the hospital; I'll just wait until she comes home.

I realized that the pillar of salt fit me like a glove.

Important lessons in life are seldom cheap. Lot's wife lost her life. Her tuition was expensive, and what amazes me most is that Lot still didn't get it. (That's why most men belong in the "slow learners" class.)

Day-to-day decisions led to family destruction, and the downward spiral had just begun. The poison of this paradise lived on in the hearts of Lot's only remaining possessions—his daughters. Earlier they watched as their father attempted to negotiate a trade: their purity for his preservation (see Genesis 19:8). Lot was willing to trade his daughters to the men of Sodom for the safety of two angelic guests. He should have offered his protection, but instead he attempted to trade his daughters' innocence for his immunity.

And you think you come from a dysfunctional family!

Can you imagine? In the eyes of these two girls, their mother had been lost because her godless desires had ruled her heart. Their father had fallen because his character had no compass.

Another lesson had been learned.
His daughters had taken note, and now it was their turn.

Lot's daughters could be no more committed to character than their parents before them had been. A trade was about to be made. In this case it would not be principle for prosperity (as their father had chosen), for these daughters were lonely and childless. Instead, their choice would be integrity for motherhood, principle for parenthood (see Genesis 19:30–38). Their plan included drunkenness, seduction, and incest with the very man who had been designed to be their moral role model: their father.

I can't help but wonder if Lot ever looked back, as his wife did. Not with envy for the past, but with remorse for the present. I wonder if he ever reflected on how the choices he had made had carved a character path that his daughters would follow. Maybe it never crossed his mind. Not because he was a bad person, but because he was a misguided one—a Hollywood tourist without a map, a kite without a tail, a ship without a rudder.

Lot's formula to fulfillment had been learned within the walls of his tent and written on the formative hearts of his children. So now an intoxicated father would serve their purpose; now the father of their character would become the father of their children.

The priorities of a parent became the principles of a child.
Like I said, it doesn't have to be this way.

A Lot to Lose

How did a distinguished family become a dysfunctional family? Easy (this isn't rocket science). It was a matter of misguided principles and mistaken priorities. Unfortunately, Lot is not alone.

Some years ago we interviewed a very prominent evangelist and his previously promiscuous daughter. While he had been saving the world, she had been selling her body. They had been estranged and living in two different worlds...socially, spiritually, and sexually. She left home at age seventeen, neglected by a father who had traded his daughter for his ministry. You see, there were pulpits to fill and sermons to preach. He needed to be needed; she needed to be loved. He found his acclaim as a preacher; she found hers as a prostitute.

Lowell Lundstrom was a successful evangelist. Invitations were numerous, churches were filled, and altars were crowded. Little did anyone know that after they left the pew and he left the pulpit, Lowell would drive the sin-filled streets of that town searching for his wayward daughter. His heart wept as he drove deeper and deeper into the "sex for sale" section of the inner city. In his heart, she was his princess. On the streets, she was someone's prostitute.

As we discussed the events that led up to this tragedy, Lowell was candid and contrite. With his daughter sitting beside him on the set, he openly admitted that during that time in his life, he had preached on the significance of family, but he had practiced the importance of his profession. Left in the emotional backdraft of his inconsistency, his daughter had found others who would value her, even if for only an hour at a time. Lowell and his daughter's relationship was eventually restored, but the scars remained. Lowell wept as he recalled the error of his ways and how his actions had spoken louder than his intentions. Lowell was given a second chance. Not everyone is so fortunate.

If Lot could live his life all over again, would he make the same choices? Not likely. Would he be guided by the same principles? No way. Once he discovered the consequences of his choices, I'm sure he'd realize that...

*What our kids see in us today determines
what our kids will become tomorrow.*

As a grandfather, Lot looked carefully at a reflection of himself in a nearby pond, then deeply into the eyes of his grandchildren. He noticed a striking resemblance. Hopefully, the similarities were a matter of complexion and not a matter of conduct.

With this in mind, principle-centered parents will seek to display healthy principles, biblical priorities, and Christlike character. Why? Because what we display by our choices today, our kids will demonstrate in their behavior tomorrow. The conduct we want for them tomorrow must be evident in our words—and our walk—today.

Despite the speeches we offer at the supper table and the sermons we preach from the pulpit, our conduct still speaks louder than our curriculum. There's no question about it: When it comes to character, most lessons on character are caught—not taught.

A Lot to Gain

The lesson to be learned here is that we have a lot to lose when priorities of greed override principles of God. However, we all have a lot to gain when our walk resembles our talk. The bottom line is:

Conduct always speaks louder than curriculum.

Conduct in the Classroom

Yes, school's in session. Today. Tomorrow. Every day. Your home is the classroom and your conduct is the curriculum that your children will remember most. This is because our behavior is what will be written in their memories. That's why it's worth saying again: First we develop, and then we distribute. Sorry, but that's the way it works.

Healthy parents are likely to develop healthy kids.
That's hard to dispute.
Healthy kids are likely to become healthy adults.
That makes sense.
Healthy adults are likely to become healthy couples.
All right.
Healthy couples are likely to develop healthy families.
Okay.
The bottom line?
Healthy parents are still the best ingredients
for healthy kids.

JENNI'S TIPS FROM THE TRENCHES... TO TURN THINGS AROUND

According to Dolores Curran, author of *Traits of a Healthy Family*, hundreds of families she studied demonstrated fifteen common traits that produced healthy kids. According to Curran, a healthy family:

1. affirms and supports one another.
2. models respect for family members.
3. promotes effective communication and listening skills.
4. develops trust for one another.
5. demonstrates a sense of play and humor.
6. believes in shared responsibility.
7. teaches a moral sense of right and wrong.
8. promotes family heritage through tradition.
9. encourages interaction among family members.
10. respects the privacy of one another.
11. promotes service to others.
12. maximizes table time for communication.
13. shares leisure and fun time.
14. admits problems and seeks help.
15. lives and teaches a strong commitment to faith.[1]

It's worth repeating:
Healthy families produce healthy kids.

Now let's conclude with an example of what's happening in America today. It illustrates our need to deal more with the problem and dance less with the symptoms.

You are walking along the bank of a river. Suddenly from

the river you hear a child crying out for help. You dive into the raging waters to rescue the child. You successfully rescue the victim, but once you are back on the shore, you hear another call for help. Again, the cry is coming from the river.

The same thing happens several times, and soon a group of rescuers is pulling children from the river. After a while you can't keep up with the number of victims being swept along by the current. Finally, you realize that the situation is endless and decide to look upstream to determine why these kids are all being swept into the river.

Upstream there is a sign that reads: "Jump! Your parents did!"

We can turn things around if we become what we believe, live what we profess, and develop before we distribute. This process is one that will enable us to reap what we desire: Healthy kids living in healthy families raised by healthy parents.

When parents choose character over comfort, we demonstrate an "upstream approach" to parenting that addresses the problem rather than focusing on the endless stream of symptoms. Sure, it's not easy. But school's in session, our kids are taking notes, and their future is hanging in the balance. The exam will take place the next time their back is against the wall.

You're their teacher…want an apple?

Chapter Three

When Giving In...Is Easier Than Going On

Never Give Up. Never Resign.

Never Concede. Never Let Go. Never!

Failure is the path of least persistence.

Unknown

If at first you don't succeed,
you're probably just like the rest of us!

Unknown

Let's Talk with Jenni

If your marriage is invigorating and parenthood is exhilarating, then you can move on to the next chapter.

For the rest of us…

- Marriage is challenging. We want to reconsider.
- Parenthood is demanding. We want to retreat.

- Work is overwhelming. We want to resign.
- And getting in shape…is just plain exhausting.

You name it, I've tried it. From cross-training to Tae-Bo, I've exercised, Jazzercised, and aerobicized to the point that death sounded like a reasonable option. I've sweated to the oldies and I've strained to the "newies." I have walked, jogged, bounced, kicked, and pedaled my way through just about every exercise program you'll see advertised at 2 A.M. Know what I've got to show for it? Six videos, four books, and a $470 Visa bill!

Can you believe it? I've given each of these programs the best five days of my life, expecting abs of steel and buns of…well, you know.

I want a total body makeover…in an hour.
Is there a problem here?

Okay, I have to admit it: Maybe I didn't really give these programs a chance. I seem to do that a lot. I live in a world of instant gratification, so I want instant results. From instant millionaires to instant marriages (or both—remember Darva?), it seems that everything can be done instantly in this dot.com world. E-mail has replaced snail mail, and sending a package to my mom by overnight delivery sounds like something left over from the last millennium.

If it doesn't happen at the speed of light,
I want another option.

Not too long ago, though, I was *determined* to stick it out. Chuck had bought me a pair of maroon Rollerblade in-line skates for my birthday, so I was on a roll—literally! (What made me think I could balance on rolling shoes when I've always had a hard time balancing on stationary ones is beyond me.) So off I went. Now, in my own defense, I must say that I am a magnificent starter. I begin new projects with motivation, dedication, and determination. If you want a project started, I'm your person. If you want it completed, call Chuck.

Anyhow, my in-line skating skills were pretty shaky at first. But I was determined to stick with it. I'm sure I was quite a sight to behold as I fumbled and stumbled my way up and down the neighborhood streets wearing more padding than an NFL lineman. In fact, on several occasions my kids asked me if I could possibly find a place to skate indoors, where I would be out of sight. But that didn't deter me. *This* time I was going to persevere—I would show them. This time there would be no giving up, no turning back!

My regular route was a four-block stretch that surrounded my home. But then one fine day, with the sun shining bright and the wind to my back, I decided it was time to "kick it up a notch." After only eight days of my new exercise routine, I was feeling good, looking great, and sleeping like a log. So I thought, *If I'm seeing this much progress after skating just four blocks a day, just imagine the results I would get if I doubled it…or even tripled it! Wouldn't Richard Simmons be proud of me then!*

So off I went, feeling totally confident and quite adventurous. I rounded the corner of my neighborhood, and off I rolled to explore new territory. I felt like Christopher Columbus. I was free. It felt great! I skated along, singing to myself and enjoying the scenery. Feeling a sense of pride and achievement when I reached the highway, I turned around to survey my accomplishment and head back home.

Then it happened.

I was not prepared for what I saw looming before me. It seems that in my zest for this unparalleled challenge, I had neglected to take note of the fact that the whole journey to that point—from my driveway to the highway—had been downhill. That meant one thing: I was in serious trouble!

There I was, suddenly aware that my return home would involve going through, around, or over what looked like Mount Everest. As I looked up and evaluated that huge hill, my determination to press on evaporated like dew on a desert road. Standing there at the bottom of that virtual mountain peak, I was no longer interested in fitness or fighting flabbiness—I just wanted to be home. Right there, at the corner of Daisy Road and Highway 377, I was finished. I quit.

Cell phones were made for occasions like this. The taxi fare home cost sixteen dollars for the ride and five dollars for the tip. It's the best twenty-one dollars I've ever spent.

All the way home I told myself that I never should have started this aimless activity anyhow. After all, I was designed to be a sprinter, not a marathoner. I was built for speed, not distance. It was all Chuck's fault. He never should have given me the stupid skates in the first place! Do you know how much they cost? And besides, maroon doesn't go with anything in my closet anyway. That's when I concluded that maybe sunbathing was the sport for me.

LET'S TALK WITH CHUCK:
THE CHALLENGE OF CHANGE

Jenni demands it. I detest it. How about you?

To me, there are two kinds of people in this world: the fickle and the fixated. Jenni is the poster child for fickle people. She says change is necessary—out with the old, in with the new. What was once ours can now be yours (at a garage sale for about ten cents on the dollar). Change drives the economy; it liberates the soul. Choices are many; time is short. Jenni's motto is "I've gotta go! The mall closes at 10 P.M."

On the other hand, I represent the fixated. I resist change—even if I don't like what I have, where I'm going, or how I got here. I say keep what you've got…it could get worse. The grass may be greener on the other side of the street, but it still has to be mowed! I say bloom where you're planted. Fix the old (it may still be under warranty). Stay the course. Take your time. Check out the options. Do the research. Purchase only when necessary. Measure twice; cut once.

I know what you're thinking...
not exactly Mr. Electric, right?

Somewhere between the erratic and the enduring, your life is driven by demands, deadlines, and dirty diapers. Maybe that's you. You press on, but you want change—not change for a dollar, but change from the doldrums. You may be numb, but you're not negligent—you notice seminars that pledge to show you how to buy half of your hometown with no money down. You see commercials that promise you'll lose twenty pounds by tomorrow—in your sleep.

Now we're talking!

Jenni wants to change everything, everywhere, every day. She says that those who resist change are those who have found their residence in a rut. I, on the other hand, believe there's a lot to be said for those who stay the course, for those who go the distance. I say there's a lot to be gained on the road to perseverance.

Just ask Bill Broadhurst.

The Marathon Man

I'll never forget the day. I was driving from Baltimore to Washington, listening to the radio, when I heard Dr. D. James Kennedy tell the story of a man named Bill Broadhurst. To me, Bill's behavior defined perseverance.

Bill wanted to be a runner in the worst way, but he had a problem. When he was young, he had had surgery for a brain aneurysm, which had left him partially paralyzed. He struggled first to walk, then to jog, and finally to run—if you could call it running.

Now, Bill Broadhurst had a hero named Bill Rogers, the famous marathon runner. One day Broadhurst heard that Bill Rogers was coming to Omaha to run in a 10K charity race. All his life, Broadhurst had dreamed about running a race with his hero. Now his pain had a purpose.

Broadhurst was willing to do whatever it took to progress from dreaming to doing. This race gave him the opportunity to accomplish his ambition, to fulfill his fantasy, to define his destiny.

This was like offering...
the presidency to a pauper,

sainthood to a scoundrel,
a medical degree to a candy striper.

The day finally came. It was a misty July morning in 1981. Positioned at the starting line were twelve hundred runners. The swift were stationed at the front, the feeble to the rear, but Broadhurst held to his dream. Soon he would stand face-to-face with his hero, if not at the starting line, 6.2 miles later at the finish line.

The gun went off. It was 9:04 A.M.

Rogers ran like a deer. Broadhurst ran more like a duck. He would throw his stiff left leg forward and pivot as his right leg hit the ground. Soon it became obvious that the pack would leave Broadhurst in the dust. It didn't take long. The pack was out of sight, but Broadhurst was not out of spirit.

As expected, Rogers finished the race first, in 29.5 minutes.

Seasoned marathoners finished in about 35 to 40 minutes.

The moderate took about 50 minutes.

The mediocre needed about 70 minutes.

The maimed were still marching on.

A full 90 minutes had passed since the starter fired his pistol, but Broadhurst pressed on. He had never run this far before, and it showed. His left side was numb. He endured pain with every step, but there was purpose to his suffering. Hope remained at the center of his will. Bill Broadhurst was not about to give up, give in, or go home.

10:55 A.M.: The police had removed the barriers along the road. The spectators had scattered. The event was already history to most—but not to Broadhurst.

In his mind he saw only the finish line. On the street he heard only sarcasm. Running the race one step at a time, he couldn't help but hear the comments from kids who stood on the street corner.

"Hey, mister, they went thataway!"
Broadhurst pressed on.
"What's wrong, mister? Did you get lost?"
Broadhurst focused on the prize, not the pain.
"Give it up, Gimp. Call it a day, Cripple."
Say what they would, Broadhurst had a mission.

Bill Broadhurst had heard it all by then. What about you? Have you heard the crowd's comments lately?

At school, your child failed third grade.
You hear: "What kind of parent are you?"
At the bank, your funds are running low.
You hear: "Nobody else has these kinds of problems."
At home, there is an empty chair at the supper table.
You hear: "He's never coming back, you know."
At work, you are berated by the boss.
You hear: "Quit now, before it's too late."
In the mirror, you can't help but notice the worst.
You hear: "You used to be so cute. Now look at you."
At church, you are reminded that you're a sinner.
You hear: "And you call yourself a Christian?"

Sometimes the road of life seems like an uphill marathon. You're running low on optimism. You know that there has to be a way out of the wilderness, but it feels like August in Arizona with no reprieve in sight.

Bill Broadhurst pressed on. How about you?

By this time, the streets were jammed with cars, but Broadhurst wasn't deterred. He took to the sidewalk and pressed on toward his mark. The pain was unbearable. His body said to quit, but his will said, "Never."

Suddenly, the tide began to turn.

Some of the onlookers were still milling around on the sidewalk where the finish line had once stood. Somehow they began to recognize Broadhurst's situation. As more and more of them realized what was happening, they began to applaud this courageous warrior. It was as though Broadhurst's determination represented a part of each of them that had always wanted to stay the course when the wind blew hard but didn't.

Jeers became cheers. Applause was heard from their hands, and praise was heard from their lips: "You can do it! Keep going! Don't give up now!"

Surrounded by his newfound supporters, Broadhurst was now within sight of the end. The finish line had been removed, but the image remained in his mind. His body was numb, but his resolve remained strong.

Then, almost magically, Broadhurst's spirit began to soar as he caught sight of his hero.

From an alley, a group of people emerged. At the center of this circle was Bill Rogers, who was returning from the celebration activities and was wearing the gold medal. The two men's paths converged.

Pupil and professor came face-to-face.

Broadhurst collapsed at the finish line into the arms of Bill

Rogers, and Rogers was quick to see the significance of the situation. He removed the gold medal from his own neck and placed it around the neck of this weary warrior. Rogers whispered into Broadhurst's ear, "You're the hero of this race. You deserve the medal."

Enjoy life when you can. Endure life when you must, so that in all things you "run with endurance the race that is set before [you]" (Hebrews 12:1).

Bill Broadhurst didn't come to run a race; he came to *finish* it.

Now let me ask you again…how about you?

The Temptation to Quit

It's easy to quit. There's always a good reason or a contract with an escape clause. It's effortless: no strain, no struggle, no sweat. From responsibilities to relationships, if things aren't "working out," we cut our losses and move on. If this isn't the trip we signed up for, then there must be a Plan B.

When I'm feeling this way, that's when God whispers to me, "Don't forget the eleventh commandment."

I check my Bible. I'm short one commandment. I find only ten, so I ask, "What's the eleventh commandment?"

"Thou shalt not quit." It's called a sin of omission, and it's critical for the sake of your future…and the sake of your family.

Our kids are watching, so…

- when we decide to quit jogging, they want to quit soccer.
- when we decide to quit our job, they want to quit school.
- when we decide to quit our marriage, they want to quit trying. Period.

Our kids live in a world that is filled with unlimited options and choices. They live in an ADD (Attention Deficit Disorder) world that constantly changes. However, we believe that persistence is important for a purposeful parent and our kids need:

- parents who model perseverance.
- parents who cheer for them as they run their race.
- parents who dare them to dream...again and again.
- parents who feed their faith and challenge their fears.
- parents who remind them that the rewards go to those who endure.
- parents who teach them that discouragement is a tool of the Deceiver.

The most important life lessons are taught to our kids when they're on the sidelines watching their opponents stand on the podium. Character development for children (and for parents) is forged on the field during a 42–7 loss, when the trip home is filled with silence. When we notice a tear running down the cheek of a fourteen-year-old boy who left everything he has on the field and has no desire to return next week to pick it up again.

Character is developed by trial, not by triumph.

Failure is something we can all identify with...time and time again. Although we live in a world that glorifies success, few of us will ever wear a diamond crown on our head or a championship ring on our finger. We credit successful people with having "God-given" talent, inherited intelligence, or just plain luck. Yet we fail to account for perseverance. If we looked behind the accomplishment, we would see that it took most people years of practice—to become an "overnight success."

That's why we need to teach our kids:

> ## Principle #3:
> *Never Give Up. Never Resign.*
> *Never Concede. Never Let Go. Never!*

Success Found the Old-Fashioned Way

After years of scanning the parenting section of our local Barnes & Noble, scouring the fine print of the *Wall Street Journal,* and seeking the advice of many a millionaire, Jenni and I have found the best prescription for success—and it was offered by Solomon.

Now, I wish I could make Solomon's words sound more spiritual, more cosmopolitan, or more cultured, but...well... here we go. Roll your eyes if you must. Sigh if you will. But the wisest man on earth put it this way: "Go to the ant, you sluggard! Consider her ways and be wise" (Proverbs 6:6).

The ant? That's right: the persistent, purposeful, persevering ant. If an ant's mound is disturbed, all the ants rally for the cause and immediately begin to work. Without delay, they organize, form lines, assign tasks, and begin the rebuilding process. They never quit. They never give up. They never slow down.

If our home is dirty, our office is disorganized, or our life is in disarray, we throw our hands up and say, "What's the use? I quit!"

The Difference between Doers and Dreamers

In 1962, a landmark research project was conducted, the results of which were published in a journal article entitled "Cradles of Eminence." The study focused on the lives of 413 famous and exceptionally accomplished individuals. The researchers, headed by the husband and wife team of Victor and Mildred Goertzel, spent years looking for the one common denominator that might account for such greatness.

After examining a number of factors, they found that 392 of the 413 individuals (about 95 percent) had overcome extremely difficult personal or family circumstances. The Goertzels determined that, more than any other factor, perseverance was the one character trait that stood at the center of the greatness of these people. They were forged by fire. They were battered but not broken, scarred but unwilling to surrender. Tempered by life's difficulties, they became strong, stable, and resistant to setbacks.[1]

Decades ago, a friend of Thomas Edison's was consoling him after another attempt to perfect the electric lightbulb had proven unsuccessful. In response, Edison replied, "I am not discouraged, because every wrong attempt discarded is another step forward."

Not so long ago, a paper-cup salesman named Ray worked endless hours throughout his seventeen-year career with the Lily Tulip Company. One day he took a risk and left the security of a steady paycheck to start a milk shake–machine company. Though he experienced some success along the way, disappointment was a daily challenge. On his wall was a plaque that read:

Press On

Nothing in the world can take the place of persistence.
Talent will not...nothing is more common than
unsuccessful individuals with talent.
Genius will not...unrewarded genius is almost a proverb.
Education will not...the world is full of educated derelicts.
Persistence and determination alone are omnipotent.

Then one day, with his milk shake–machine in hand, Ray made a sales call to a small hamburger shop in San Bernardino. He met a couple of brothers who were flipping burgers, and he liked what he saw. He convinced the brothers that he could increase their sales if they let him franchise their shop. This concept was unheard-of to them, but the brothers agreed. Ray Kroc was fifty-two years old at the time—and built McDonald's into a billion-dollar business in just twenty-two years. He owes his success not to talent, genius, or education, but solely to perseverance.

It's Time to Dream Again

Remember that time in your life when your dream defined your day? No, I'm not talking about a fleeting fancy or a passing aspiration. I'm talking about something much deeper. I'm talking about a dream that feels more like an insatiable appetite, one that isn't satisfied with a full stomach. For you, this dream is more than a race to run; it's a mandate from the Master.

Unfortunately, your dreams have faded. Like Bill Broadhurst, you began the race. Unlike him, your passion passed, your excitement lapsed, and the race was over for you before you crossed the finish line.

Maybe there was a good reason. Maybe someone told you things, such as:

you're too young	*or*	you're too old
you're undereducated	*or*	you're overeducated
you're not a man	*or*	you're not a woman
you're a minority	*or*	you're a majority
you're married	*or*	you're single

The list never ends. But remember, others have been told the same. For example, expert opinion told Mr. Bell:

Well-informed people know it is impossible to transmit the human voice over wires and that, were it possible to do so, the thing would be of no practical value. (*Boston Post*, 1865)

Did you hear that, Alexander?

I learned the value of perseverance firsthand when "expert opinion" polls concluded that good ol' Chuck would never graduate from high school and the likelihood of going to college was about the same as being NASA's first man on the moon. I demanded a recount!

Sometime later, the "experts" revised their opinion and concluded that I had "potential." At the time I thought "potential" was an honor, but over time I began to realize it was more of an insult. *Potential* suggests that the resources are present but are as dormant as a black bear in December. Applying effort, energy, and endurance is what made the difference for me.

Add a pound of perseverance to an ounce of potential, and now you've got the ingredients for success.

Need some more examples?

Winston Churchill

…failed the sixth grade and did not become the prime minister of England until he was a sixty-two-year-old senior citizen, and only then after a lifetime of setbacks and defeats.

Albert Einstein

…didn't speak until he was four years of age and didn't read until he was seven. His teachers described him as mentally slow, unsociable, and unfocused. He was expelled from school and was refused admittance to the Zurich Polytechnic School.

Walt Disney

…was fired by a newspaper editor because he lacked any original ideas for stories. He was also forced to declare bankruptcy several times before he eventually built Disneyland in California.

Ludwig van Beethoven

…preferred playing his own compositions instead of improving his technique and handled the violin so awkwardly that his teachers concluded he was hopeless as a composer.

Michael Jordan

...was cut from the basketball team his sophomore year, but a coach who believed in him worked with Michael before and after school, developing his skills. Eventually, Jordan went on to make the varsity basketball team in high school, but not until his senior year. In the NBA, he earned ten scoring championships. The next closest to him was Wilt Chamberlain, with seven.

The list goes on. Theodor Geisel was rejected more than seventy times before he could find a publisher to print his first Dr. Seuss book. Henry Ford went broke five times before he finally succeeded. The parents of opera tenor Enrico Caruso wanted him to become an engineer because his teachers concluded that he had no vocal talent.

Furthermore, Scripture is full of examples of people who persevered. Examples from the lives of Joseph, Moses, Noah, Job, David, Peter, and Paul offer purpose for those who wish to persevere and drive for those who are discouraged.

I wish I could tell you that perseverance alone guarantees the prize. However, the truth is that you may do all your homework and still not be accepted into Harvard. You may resist every dessert on the tray and still not fit into a size-three dress. But those who persevere achieve the reward of a deep and determined character.

Why persevere?
Because it's time to teach our kids that
it's better to lose by defeat than by default!

Jenni's Tips from the Trenches...
to Turn Things Around

1.   Model perseverance.

How can I ask my kids to persevere in the classroom when I'm packing my in-line skates away in the attic? Whether it relates to staying in shape, staying on a diet, or staying in a marriage, it's important to set and achieve short-term goals. Just like many of you, every year I try to reorganize my life on December 31. I start out to accomplish *all* of my physical, marital, financial, and spiritual goals by the same time next year. But by February, I'm exhausted—not exhilarated.

Instead of trying to achieve a total life makeover, set one short-term goal and accomplish it. For example, my doctor wants me to walk for thirty minutes, three times a week. I've committed to this goal for one month. At the end of the month, I will celebrate my success and redefine my goal for the following month. Because nothing motivates like success, this strategy is a great way to achieve your long-term goals—one step at a time. Your kids will see you modeling this behavior and will be encouraged to persevere toward their own goals.

2.   Pray with persistence.

Maybe you know the heartache of having a prodigal son or daughter. Maybe you know the pain of having a broken marriage or a wayward spouse. What should we do when we are faced with these kinds of situations? We should pray with persistence.

In Luke 11, after Jesus had finished teaching his disciples the Lord's Prayer, He then shared with them the Parable of the Persistent Friend:

"Which of you shall have a friend, and go to him at midnight and say to him, 'Friend, lend me three loaves; for a friend of mine has come to me on his journey, and I have nothing to set before him'; and he will answer from within and say, 'Do not trouble me; the door is now shut, and my children are with me in bed; I cannot rise and give it to you'? I say to you, though he will not rise and give to him because he is his friend, yet because of his persistence he will rise and give him as many as he needs." (vv. 5–8)

Even though the friend may not get out of bed to provide food for his neighbor *simply because they are friends,* he will do it because of his friend's *persistence.* Is God trying to tell us something here?

I believe in the power of prayer. On some occasions I have experienced an answer almost immediately after I whispered the prayer. In other cases, I'm still praying, still believing, and still persevering. I pray every day for my kids—for their safety, their salvation, and their future. Each day I pray for Chuck, asking God to continue to equip him as the husband, father, and spiritual leader of our family. And I know that Chuck gets up early every day to spend time with the Lord before heading off to the studio.

So let me encourage you to pray persistently, expectantly, and faithfully for whatever is on the top of your prayer list. You can rely on the fact that God answers prayer.

3. Dare to dream again.

Let's go back to the days when you used to dream. What happened? Perhaps there are good reasons why your dreams were placed on the shelf, but maybe today the Lord is saying that times have changed, circumstances are different, and people are ready. I love Jeremiah 29:11, where God says, "'For I know the plans I have for you,' declares the LORD, 'plans to prosper you and not to harm you, plans to give you hope and a future'" (NIV). This verse says to me that God wants us to realize our dreams.

It's always easier to sit on the sidelines and list the reasons why we can't do something. Maybe God is whispering to you right now: *It's time to leave the stands, cross the chalk line, and get in the game. This is your day; this is your destiny. Put your hand in Mine, and we'll do it together.*

Maybe you have always wanted to go back to school or start a small business from your home. Let me encourage you to huddle with your family, dust off that wayward dream, and talk about how you can take a small (but significant) step toward accomplishing that goal together. It's never too late to start fulfilling your own dream and modeling for your children how they can accomplish their dreams. By sharing your dream and making a family commitment to accomplish it, you give each member of your family a small piece of the puzzle that they can contribute. This gives them a sense of accomplishment and gives you a sense of accountability.

4.   An activity started is an activity finished.

Whether it's Monopoly, a paper route, or varsity basketball, we have a family rule: If you start it, you finish it. Period.

For a couple of years, our family played a card game called Crazy Eights after supper. On most nights it lasted only about ten minutes, but there were occasions when it seemed like nobody was ever going to win. It got to be fun, because no matter how bad we *all* wanted to quit, we knew that the rule was "a game started is a game finished." We played till the end...even if it felt like it might kill us!

And we've found that a lesson learned at the supper table became a standard lived out on the soccer field. Five games into a ten-game season, with a record of one win and four losses, Courtney wanted to call it quits. The same rule applied: "A season started is a season finished." Courtney completed the soccer season. We tell our kids when they start a sport that they've made a commitment to complete the season and follow through with everything the coach expects them to do between the first whistle and the final buzzer. Their teammates are counting on them, so unless they told the coach up front, "I'm only going to play for this team as long as it's fun and as long as we're winning," no matter what the outcome, they're in it till the end.

5.   Celebrate a completed season, not just a championship season.

There's an old saying: "To the winner goes the spoils." In our home we believe that "to the finisher goes the spoils." If you finish, you're a champion. Anyone can begin a race, but not everyone will finish it. In our home, rewards go to those who *compete* and to those who *complete!*

Simply completing a season may seem small to some, but the lesson is significant. If completing a season is celebrated, then your children, in every activity, at the end of every season, come home winners. That's what I call bringing out the winner in your kids! And at the same time, they will learn the importance of finishing what they start.

6.   Define your goals; then share your goals.

I remember Chuck once telling me about a Harvard study that concluded that only 3 percent of Harvard graduates had clearly defined goals. He then added that the 3 percent who had taken the time to set goals were ten times more productive than the other 97 percent. When I set goals for myself, it's certainly true that I'm more productive.

Goals kept to oneself are secret desires. Goals shared with others become stated destinations. People don't pack their bags, load the car, and begin the drive toward a family vacation without knowing where they're going!

Decide where you want to go. Share it with your family. Post it on the refrigerator.

Then pack your bags. Get in the car. And don't give in. Don't give up. Don't turn around…until you arrive.

Chapter Four

WHEN LITTLE WHITE LIES...BEGIN TO COLOR YOUR CHARACTER

It's Never Right to Do Wrong.

There's one way to find out if a man is honest—ask him.
If he says yes, you know he is a crook.

GROUCHO MARX

Honesty pays, but it doesn't seem to pay enough
to suit some people.

KIN HUBBARD

LET'S TALK WITH JENNI

WELL, IT'S TIME YOU KNEW THE TRUTH about me: I was a perfect child. I made my bed, I put away my clothes, and I even turned out the lights when I left a room.

I followed the rules.

I obeyed my parents.

I went to Sunday school.

I did the right thing.

In fact, I felt it was my personal responsibility to promote Truth, Justice, and the American Way. I was the hall monitor, the teacher's pet, the class tattletale, and a card-carrying member of the Polite Police. (And I had no idea why I always ate lunch by myself in the cafeteria!) While everyone else was at recess, I was doing extra-credit work, cleaning the chalkboard, or conducting a survey.

In college, my roommates attended parties; I attended prayer meetings. The other kids challenged the dean of students, the campus police, and the college president; I was a Republican. My classmates followed the theories of Plato, Freud, Marx, and Darwin; I followed the theology of Jesus. I was a certifiable Jesus Freak and had a leather-bound, red-letter edition of the *King James Bible* to prove it! Sure of my convictions, steadfast in my faith, and unwavering in my values, I could have been a poster child for the Moral Majority. Back then I had only two shoes in my closet—and both were named "Goody."

Well, guess what? This perfect little child grew up to become a perfect little adult. Isn't that amazing? I know that Chuck is amazed every time I remind him of this!

So when it came time for me to progress from marriage to motherhood, I was enthusiastic about passing on my "perfection" to my children. It was the least I could do. That way they could carry on this heritage of perfection from generation to generation—as long as Chuck's genes didn't get in the way! I thought to myself, *How fortunate these children are to have* me, *the model of perfection, as their mother!*

Then reality set in.

It's true when they say, "Out of the mouths of babes...." In my case, it couldn't have been more accurate. In fact, it took the voice of my child (actually, I think it was Chuck's child) to set me straight and show me how high (or how low) my standards of integrity really were:

"Mommy, why did you tell that person on the phone that you were busy when you were just watching TV?"

Well, honey...

"Mommy, why didn't you tell Daddy about your new red shoes when he asked if you bought anything at the mall today?"

Sometimes it's okay if...

"Mommy, why do we have so many pens and pencils here from your office?"

You don't always...

"Mommy, why do we only buckle our seat belts when you see a police car?"

Oh, never mind...it's time for you to go outside and play!

Then I have to ask myself why it's not unusual to hear about people who...

- return clothing for a refund after it's been worn.
- switch a size-eight suit top to go with a size-ten suit bottom in the dressing room.
- tell the beggar on the street that they have no money when their wallet is full.
- fail to return the five-dollar bill when the cashier gives them too much change.
- "forget" to report that extra income each year on April 15.

White Lies Become Willful Compromise

Somewhere along the way, we let our guard down. A door that was once shut, locked, and bolted is now cracked open ever so slightly. The deceiver has his toe in the door of our integrity, and he's whispering to us:

- Everybody's doing it…
- It's no big deal…
- Just this once…
- They'll never notice…
- What's the harm…
- God understands…

Excuses. Compromises. Explanations.

Soon we become Plan B people living Plan B parenting before our children. It goes like this: "Don't have sex before marriage! *But if you do,* use a condom." "Don't drink alcohol. *But if you do,* make sure you don't drink and drive." You get the idea.

Can we really promote integrity in the lives of our kids when we encourage them to have Plan B in their back pockets? Mixed messages lead our kids to one conclusion: If our parents aren't committed to Plan A, why should we be?

You know, I've learned a lot since my hall monitor days:

- I've learned that being the right kind of person makes it easier to do the right kinds of things. That's why God always builds people from the inside out.
- I've learned that there's always a good reason to cut corners, but there are a lot of better reasons not to.

- And I've learned that *small compromises* produce *large consequences.*
- I've also learned that if the devil can't make you bad, he'll make you busy. Because when you're busy, doing what's "easy" always comes before doing what's right.

Oh yeah, as I've grown older, I've also grown wiser. I've discovered that creative minds are rarely tidy. That fact alone gives me a lot of free time!

Let's Talk with Chuck

*Integrity is doing the right thing,
regardless of the circumstances,
in spite of the costs,
whatever the consequences.*

Most of us view integrity as an all-or-nothing quality. Clergy have it; criminals don't. Actually, both are capable of telling little white lies. Most of us see integrity as a quality that is developed in ten-pound increments. Actually, integrity is developed one ounce at a time: at the grocery store, in the dressing room, on the phone—when nobody's looking. Most of us believe that unprincipled people lose their integrity by the mile rather than by the foot—over big-ticket items and million-dollar deals. Actually, integrity is lost at the same rate it is gained—one ounce at a time. But Jenni's right. When you add yesterday's compromises to today's, collectively they can sink a ship…in no time.

Shipwrecked

Claims were made.
Deadlines were established.
Guarantees were given.

But they failed to account for one small problem—the ice.

Nothing but frozen water, but it brought her to her knees…and left her to lie at the bottom of the frigid North Atlantic, 12,468 feet below sea level. It also sent countless passengers into a nautical nightmare and over fifteen hundred souls to a premature maritime grave.

Go beyond the movie, the diamond pendant, and the love story between Jack and Rose. Go to the real lesson to be learned aboard this luxury liner. If we miss this point, we're likely to sink our parental prospects as well.

Look carefully, 41 degrees north and 50 degrees west. Make your way beyond the two and a half miles of frigid blue saltwater. Buried beneath the mud, hidden by coral and guarded by marine life, lies the most immense ship that had ever been built. The year was 1912. It took fifteen thousand yard workers seven million man-hours to construct this opulent symbol of power and prestige.

She was the unsinkable. She was the majestic.
She was the RMS Titanic.

For years, the most widely held theory about the *Titanic's* sinking was that she hit an iceberg so immense that it cut a massive gash deep below the waterline on the port side of this proud, 882-foot ocean liner. However, an international team of divers and scientists came to a different conclusion. The truth was exposed by sound waves used to probe the wreckage and was later visually confirmed through the eyes of a submarine named Alvin and her remote camera. Rather than a huge gash, the gateway for destruction was actually more like a calculated incision made by a seasoned cardiologist.

Their discovery? The damage was small, but the outcome was severe. Instead of the large gash they had expected, the divers found six narrow slits that cut across several watertight compartments. Together, these slits accounted for only twelve square feet of disfigured iron.

Relatively speaking, the damage was nominal when compared to the number of square miles of steel that made up the ship. But collectively, those small blemishes sank the largest moveable object on the seas at that time.

As a result,

- a widow grieved the loss of her husband.
- a child grieved the loss of his father.
- a family grieved the loss of their lineage.

How could damage so minute create consequences so far-reaching?

Just ask David.

Following his incredible defeat of Goliath, David appeared to be unsinkable. In his day, he was the symbol of power and prestige. But there was a problem below the waterline. Although David was skillful enough to slaughter a giant on a hillside, he was powerless to resist a woman by the poolside (see 2 Samuel 11).

It began with an innocent stroll late one night when David couldn't sleep. His troops were on the battlefield, and his eyes were on a potential minefield. During his walk, David discovered a woman named Bathsheba on a rooftop, taking a bath. His discovery led to a decision. His glance became a goal. He made choices. Invisible to most, these choices clouded his conscience and scarred his character. Soon lust became adultery, adultery became murder...and his relationship with God went from sacred to scarred.

So many times before, David had taken the high road. But not this time. He quickly progressed from looking to lusting, from fantasy to fulfillment. Satan had his foot in the door. One small slit was found in the armor of David's character, and like the *Titanic,* he began to take on water.

You know what I'm talking about. Maybe you've been there yourself.

Rules of Engagement

A coworker catches your eye. He tells you that you look good in blue. He notices your perfume. He listens when you speak. He remembers your birthday. You find a reason to talk together and then work together. You bring him home with you—first in your mind and then in your heart. No one seems to notice, but the Titanic is in trouble. You send out an SOS to your husband. But he's twenty miles away...on a golf course.

There's no response.

According to some researchers, as many as 25 percent of women and 33 percent of men will be unfaithful during the course of their marriage—and will admit to it.[1] First we rationalize; then we justify. Instead of raising our integrity, we find it more convenient to lower our standards. Our guard falls and so does our faith. Satan is in the process of sinking another marriage. Unfortunately, when a marriage sinks, the kids go down with the ship.

> *But it's never too late to do the right thing.*
> *It's never too late to turn things around.*

While his ship was on its way down, David looked up. He concluded that no one is too wrong to do right. No one is too bad to do good. No one is too lost to find grace. David confronted his behavior. He confessed his sin and experienced God's grace. He found an oasis in the desert.

> *With God...*
> *every thoughtless mistake*
> *every loveless marriage*
> *every rebellious child*
> *every hurting heart*
> *and every sinking ship*
> *has a lifeboat.*

Integrity begins with truth in our hearts and ends with action in our homes. It will keep a train on its tracks. It provides a moral compass to help parents and kids navigate the "relative" world we live in. Integrity will cost us a lot to live by, but will cost us even more to live without. It's hard to define, but easy to spot. It is applicable at home, at school, and at the office. Integrity—or the lack thereof—can define you or destroy you. It's an issue of will, not wisdom. It's developed, not demanded. A lack of integrity can turn the unacceptable into the tolerable, the prohibited into the permissible.

Integrity is the backbone of character, and that's why we need to teach our kids:

> ## PRINCIPLE #4:
> *It's Never Right to Do Wrong.*

Throw Me a Lifesaver

Some people mistake reputation for integrity. But they're cousins, not twins. Reputation is external and is based on what people think of us. Integrity, on the other hand, is internal and is based on who we are when nobody's looking.

Reputation can vary by person, place, time, and situation. For example, your spouse sees you as a loving provider, while at the same time your manager sees you as a ruthless salesman. Both may be true; both may be rewarded. But integrity is internal. It's a moral compass that cuts across circumstances, costs, and consequences. It describes what we do, not what we claim to be.

But some people say they have a defense, grounds for dismissal. Some of those defenses are better than others.

During twenty years of private practice as a psychologist, I've heard it all. From the mouth of an inmate I heard, "It was the drugs. You should be locking up the drug dealers who sold them to me!" From an incorrigible adolescent I heard, "If my father had been home more often I wouldn't have stolen all of his stuff." From the lips of a promiscuous woman I heard, "If someone would have loved me when I was growing up, I wouldn't have looked for it in the arms of a paying client."

We intellectualize, rationalize, and spiritualize. And when

that doesn't work, we simply justify. I've sat with many a wayward husband and heard many a weary defense explaining an affair and the beliefs behind the behavior. It typically begins with "I didn't really love her when we got married." It doesn't take long until those words are closely followed by:

- "This will be better for the kids, you know."
- "This will give us both a chance to be happy."
- "I've prayed about it and God understands."

The slippery slope...at its worst.

I heard these very words from a successful pastor whose future was earmarked by the denomination as having "headquarters" potential. I've had a lot of difficult days while in clinical practice, but none more painful than the afternoon when this pastor told his wife and three children about his decision to leave them and the church...for another lover. His wife was crushed; his children were crippled. They sat motionless, tears filling their eyes and fears filling their hearts. Their father's faith—the faith he preached about every Sunday morning, the faith they cut their spiritual teeth on—was now about as appetizing as a bowl of artificial fruit.

Integrity.
A pastor assigned to teach it
was a person unable to live it.

While parents do their best to hold the moral banner high, others—from the pastorate to the presidency—have let their children down. Time and time again.

Modern-Day Mishaps

As far as presidents go, most have concluded that William Jefferson Clinton was one of the most gifted of all time. Many credit him with being a consummate communicator. Indeed, he was a master at connecting with the American public. But though he did much for our country's economy, he did little for our country's integrity. In fact, he lowered the bar to a new low in 1999.

Ability is a blessing; character is a choice.

In Clinton's case, "truth" was determined by definition. Lawyers dueled, journalists investigated, and spin doctors spun their "strategic misinformation." Leno and Letterman had him for lunch, and the country grew weary. As the truth unfolded, Republicans called his behavior "perjury" while Democrats labeled it "trivial." And as the debate raged on, few noticed a wife and daughter sitting on the emotional sidelines, with hearts in hand and home hanging in the balance. With two years left in office, this ship took on water and barely made it back to port. At the same time, our kids watched and took notes. And many of them concluded that right and wrong are no longer absolutes.

But Clinton wasn't the first…

More than twenty-five hundred years ago, this falsehood was designed to save a man's life—not just politically but literally. Once again, it all came down to "the definition": six inches of truth and a half-foot of lie, not once but twice. Fearful for his life, he told the pharaoh that his wife was his sister. Her name is Sarai; his is Abraham. While his faith became famous (see Hebrews 11:8–19), his character became flawed (see Genesis 12 and 20).

In our world today, headlines give gruesome details and tragic stories of broken promises, broken dreams, and broken hearts. Families are constantly bombarded with reports ranging from corporate capitalists who trade inside information to misguided ministers who fumble their affections.

First we ask ourselves, "Who's next?" Then we say, "If they couldn't keep their behavior on the moral plumb line, then how can I?" Finally we conclude, "If everybody's doing it, why can't I?"

This lack of integrity has shipwrecked many sailors. And now, as our kids drift on the sea, we faintly hear their cries: "Would somebody please throw me a lifesaver?"

JENNI'S TIPS FROM THE TRENCHES... TO TURN THINGS AROUND

1. Examine your beliefs. They determine your behavior.

Behavior follows beliefs. Period. The majority of the time parents focus on a child's misguided behavior, but we need to back up the boat and examine the underlying *beliefs* that form the birthplace for that behavior. They sound like this:

- "I can't help it. It's just the way I was brought up."
- "Nobody reports all their income."
- "The company won't miss a few tools from the shop."
- "If I don't lie for the boss, he'll fire me."
- "If the customer doesn't ask, it's not my job to tell him."
- "What's the problem? Everybody pads their expense report."
- "If the cashier gives me too much change, I see it as a gift from God."

We place compromise above conviction when we believe that the end justifies the means. Character takes a backseat to convenience and integrity suffers another slash below the waterline, where most people believe it will go unnoticed.

To a wayward church in Rome, the apostle Paul said, "Do not conform any longer to the pattern of this world, but be transformed by the renewing of your mind" (Romans 12:2, NIV). The bottom line? A renewed faith within the heart of a parent produces renewed beliefs within the mind of a parent. The apostle Paul implies that renewed beliefs will result in righteous behavior. He also reminds us of a fundamental principle of human conduct: Beliefs determine behavior.

An Example from Chuck

I was selling our car. I advertised it as a "Cream Puff: one owner, driven to church on Sundays." Well, it was true…as long as you didn't count the trips taken Monday through Saturday. I figured, *Hey, they'll never notice. They'll kick the tires. They'll pop the hood. They'll take it for a spin around the block. Sold.*

Jenni asks me if I told them that the transmission slips.

I say they didn't ask.

Jenni asks me if I told them the wipers don't work.

I say they didn't notice.

Jenni asks me if I told them that the spare tire in the trunk is flat.

I say they didn't look.

Jenni asks me about the condition of my integrity.

I must admit that I needed a moral makeover.

2. Teach by example. "Well done" is better than "well said."

In a letter to Titus, his "partner and fellow worker" (2 Corinthians 8:23, NIV), the apostle Paul once again addressed the issue of teaching integrity. The method he recommended in the first century is what we call "modeling" in the twenty-first century:

> In everything set them an example by doing what is good. In your teaching show integrity, seriousness and soundness of speech. (Titus 2:7–8, NIV)

Teach by example. Model what you desire. For our children to develop character of integrity, they must first see the integrity of our character. In a world that endorses situational ethics and moral flexibility, the apostle Paul reminds us to "set them an example by doing." Like Paul, I believe that the most meaningful classroom your children will ever attend is located in your home.

An Example from Chuck

Jenni asks me, "Why is there a radar detector on the dashboard of our car?"

I say, "Everybody's got one...we live in Texas."

Jenni asks me, "Do you plan on breaking the law by speeding today?"

I feel like a deer caught in the headlights of an eighteen-wheeler.

Enough said.
Your kids are watching.

3.   It's never right to do wrong.

Integrity is never easy to initiate. It's even harder to maintain. Tests of our integrity will occur when we least expect them:

- at the cash register
- in the dressing room
- on an expense account
- on a tax return
- when no one's looking.

Everyone knows that when it comes to parenting, consistency is our best ally (unless of course we're consistently inconsistent). The consistency of our integrity is equally critical. In all probability, sometime today your character will be challenged.

What will you do?
Abraham Lincoln said, "Pay the price, and reap the rewards."

Throughout his administration, Abraham Lincoln was under fire, especially during the scarring years of the Civil War. Although he knew he would make errors in office, he resolved never to compromise his integrity. His resolve was so strong that he once declared, "I desire so to conduct the affairs of this administration that if at the end, when I come to lay down the reins of power, if I have lost every other friend on earth, I shall at least have one friend left, and that friend shall be down inside of me."[2]

He determined that it's never right to do wrong.
Not even a little wrong. It costs too much.

The apostle Paul challenged the church in Corinth. They wanted their spirituality to be graded on a curve. But he reminded them that "a little leaven leavens the whole lump" (1 Corinthians 5:6).

> *Never compromise yourself.*
> *Not today. Not tomorrow.*
> *Never.*

You're the most influential role model your kids will ever have. They need you to model integrity, teach integrity, and reward integrity when they demonstrate it.

An Example from Chuck

Jenni asks me, "Why didn't you come to a complete stop at the stop sign?"

I say, "I didn't see anybody else at the intersection, so why stop?"

Jenni asks me, "Did you notice the police officer behind the tree over there?"

Jenni is really starting to bother me!

Chapter Five

When the Mirror on the Wall...Sees You As a Fixer-Upper

Believe in Your Kids—Even When

They Don't Believe in Themselves.

I always wanted to be somebody,
but I should have been more specific.

Lily Tomlin

Let's Talk with Jenni:
"Mirror, Mirror, on the Wall"

Go ahead. Admit it. We've all looked into the mirror at some time in our life and asked that magical question, "Mirror, mirror, on the wall, who's the fairest of them all?"

Unfortunately, when I was growing up all I heard was, "Not you again!"

The truth is, I was a late bloomer (my sister disputes

whether I bloomed at all). During most of my adolescence, I looked like a human pencil! In addition to a five-foot-eight figure that would make Twiggy look like Dolly Parton, I also wore Coke-bottle glasses, orthodontic headgear, and orthopedic footwear. I took "nerd" to a new level. I had everything but the plastic pocket protector.

While the other girls in my class began to resemble Snow White, I was on the fast track to becoming the human clone of Popeye's Olive Oyl. I was unknown, unpopular, and definitely uncool. Oh, don't feel sorry for me. I survived. We all do. But just like so many others, I didn't escape adolescence unscathed.

It's been thirty years, but sometimes I still feel myself reliving those agonizing feelings from my adolescence. Suddenly it's as if I'm fifteen again, and I feel that familiar sinking feeling in the pit of my stomach. I can almost hear the kids in the hallway calling me "Zipper" again.

I hid behind my locker.
I hid behind my books.
I hid behind anything that would hide my heart.

During my adolescent years, I felt the heartache of being left out and left behind. I resented my classmates, and yet I longed to be one of them. I felt lost in a foreign land. No one spoke my language—no one spoke to me period!

There were times when I longed for someone to hold that little girl inside me and tell her that she was important. That she was pretty. That she was valuable. Now, though, I want more than that for my girls. I want to protect my own daughters from those same demeaning remarks, those same embarrassing moments.

Growing up, maybe you repeated the phrase "Sticks and stones may break my bones, but names can never hurt me" as often as I did—hoping to convince yourself of its certainty. By now, though, most of us know that that's not true. After all, the wisest man that ever lived, Solomon, knew the power of the tongue. He wrote:

Death and life are in the power of the tongue. (Proverbs 18:21)

A critical comment can cut us to the core quicker than any stick and bruise our heart deeper than any stone. But as a mom, I long to provide an emotional shield for my kids. I want to give them some kind of protective covering that will guard their hearts and shelter their minds. I long for an anchor that will secure them to the knowledge that they are loved, that they are special, and that they are significant.

But how?

How does a parent instill that kind of confidence in a child? Confidence that can't be stolen, confidence that won't be traded for temporary approval. Confidence that stands strong in spite of a sarcastic remark from a peer. I'm talking about instilling confidence in our kids that's good for a season *as well as* for a life span.

"Who's the Fairest of Them All?"

Well, to find some answers, first some questions. Is self-worth passed on by genetics, developed by parents, or gained by experience? If genetics account for the presence of a trait, then how can criticism account for its departure? If circumstances can steal it, then what can a parent do to strengthen it?

For answers I turned to one of my own personal models of self-esteem—Snow White! Now stay with me here. There's more to this storybook character than silky, black hair and milky-white skin.

Sit back, relax, and travel with me to a place called "Happily Ever After." We're about to discover a few facts about this little princess. For example, this young teenager woke up every morning with a smile on her face, a song in her heart, and a desire to rise above her circumstances. Many would assume that she must have experienced the good life— a castle to live in, an adoring father to love her, and servants by the dozen to bring her warm cookies and cold milk. Not true. Snow White was raised by a wicked stepmother and quickly went from princess to pauper…from steak and potatoes to nuts and berries. Her mother died while giving birth; her father died when she was a teen. She endured constant criticism and ridicule from her stepmother.

Fateful Fact #1: Snow White was left in a forest to fend for herself.

Frightened and alone, Snow White's life was spared by the noble Huntsman, but she had little to live for. Instead of giving up, she searched for a new place to call home and discovered a seven-bedroom cottage in the woods. She made it her own, but this place came with a challenge—seven kids to care for!

Fateful Fact #2: Snow White became a caretaker to seven fun-loving dwarfs!

She met this new hardship head-on, never doubting herself or her ability to confront the challenge that stood before her. She had an unshakable confidence in herself that allowed her not only to overcome adversity, but to flourish in the midst of it.

And They All Lived Happily Ever After

Snow White's story—and the secret of her success—can teach us an important parenting principle: "Snow White's Secret to Self-Confidence." It's what made her believe that she could turn survival into success even when she had no home, no family, and no future. It's what gave her that underlying sense that her worth was deep within her heart rather than dependent upon her circumstances.

Her father made her a princess.

From the moment she was born, she was his princess. Not solely because of beauty or birthright, but because her father believed in her even when she didn't believe in herself. Snow White's self-worth was rooted deep within her heart because of the value her father placed on her and the priority he made her. Within Snow White was a belief that no matter what happened in her life, she was still his princess. A princess whose kingdom was larger than a country. A princess whose worth was greater than her possessions. She was a princess simply because her father treated her like a princess.

A little girl believed in her father, and her father believed in her. A king had his princess, and a princess had her worth.

With one hand he ruled the kingdom, but with the other he held her upon his lap, close by his heart. Not a single day went by that he didn't tell her how much he loved her. He told her that beauty is not seen with one's eyes, but is felt from one's heart. She woke with a kiss and went to bed with the same. He instilled within her the value of serving others and standing strong in the face of adversity. That's what a princess does. He taught her that it is more important to listen with your heart than with your ears. And most of all, he taught her that her worth was not determined by people's opinions but by the most important opinion of all, her own. Her father believed in her and that alone was enough for her to believe in herself. She was a princess.

A Forgotten Fact and a Pivotal Principle

An interesting thing happens when we believe in our children: They begin to believe in themselves. Self-worth isn't genetic; it's developed. It's built with building blocks given to them by their parents. Each day our kids will listen carefully to our words, and we will either hand them another building block or tear down the ones they have.

You are the mirror on your kids' wall.

So choose your words wisely. Although other kids were cruel to me when I was an underdeveloped, unbecoming, and unprepared kid, the words my parents spoke to me provided the foundation of my self-worth. Their words of love, affirmation, and encouragement made the difference in my life when the winds of criticism blew. Challenges may come, but they will never penetrate the armor of children who are royalty to their parents.

Let's Talk with Chuck: A Fairy Tale Comes Alive

So you want to be Snow White? No problem. But first we have to translate her story from a make-believe fantasy to a made-for-life reality. We need to transport Snow White from a land called "Happily Ever After" to the wheat fields of Nebraska. The real-life version might look more like this:

Age four

In the early years, you are Snow White. Your hair is as black as ebony. Your skin is as white as snow. Your castle is a Barbie Dream House, and you are the fairest of them all.

Age fourteen

You wake up! Your hair is red and your skin is freckled. The image in the mirror is plain, plump, and has pimples. You protest. This is no way to start adolescence!

Age twenty-four

The person in the mirror is now puny on the top and pudgy on the bottom. You're well educated, but not well endowed. That's okay. Eddie from the mail room loves ya, and that's all that matters, right?

Age thirty-four

You've been married to Eddie for nine years and have two hyperactive toddlers. As a woman, you feel plain. As a parent, you feel powerless. All you can say is "Thank goodness for Prozac."

Age forty-four

Eddie is moving up. He's now manager of the mail room. Your kids are in school. They need their Ritalin; you need your bifocals. It's midlife. Free time means off to school, off to work, off to the mall. And off to find yourself.

Age fifty-four

Your kids have moved out, but your parents have moved in! You need professional help: a psychologist to help you accept yourself and a plastic surgeon to help you transform yourself. They both accept insurance.

Age sixty-four

Your parents have "moved on," but your kids have moved back. Eddie appears to have permanently moved to the golf course! That's okay. It's time to prepare for retirement and time to pamper your grandchildren.

Age seventy-four

Now the kids have moved out and Eddie has "moved on." You're Snow White again…in the later years. But instead of being the fairest of them all, you don't care. Because you've just plain "had it" with them all!

Who needs a mirror anyhow?

One Last Look

I have a challenge for you. Take one more long look in the mirror and tell me what you see. Not the mirror hanging on your wall, but the one hidden deep within your heart. Don't describe the person on the outside that you've scrubbed up, dressed up, and powdered up. Look deeper. How would you describe the person on the inside of you? Deep down where no one ever looks—not even you.

Now let me ask you again. Take a long look—what do you see?

Why do I ask? Because we become what we believe. It's the self-fulfilling prophecy at its worst. Solomon put it this way:

For as he thinks in his heart, so is he. (Proverbs 23:7)

A poll conducted by George Gallup stated that 65 percent of all Protestants struggled with feelings of low self-worth and/or its consequences. Its closest relatives are depression, loneliness, isolation, fear of failure, indecision, and underproductivity.[1] Sound like anyone you know?

In the Beginning

How did we get here? When I was in graduate school, I remember hearing the results of a study that documented the fact that by the time the average child reaches five years of age, he has received 24,440 personal negative messages! Do any of these sound familiar?

- You can't go to school looking like that!

- Four A's and a C? How'd that C get in there?

- I swear you'd lose your head if it wasn't screwed on!

- Look at your room. Were you born in a barn or something?

- You don't spell *cat* with a *k*. Even your four-year-old sister knows that!

- Close the door. Do you think we're trying to air-condition all of Ohio?

- If you don't stop crying, I'll give you something to really cry about.

- ☞ Wait till your dad comes home. You're in serious trouble now!

- ☞ Why can't you be more like your older brother?

- ☞ Wipe that smirk off your face!

Here's the issue: Ninety percent of children's feelings of self-worth are based upon what *they think we think of them.*

Does anybody else see a problem here?

I'll never forget the day I met eleven-year-old Justin. His parents were at the end of their rope. Justin was about to be given his last hope—a psychologist. For most of the hour, Justin's parents exposed every sin committed by their youngest son during the past two years, from fistfights to starting fires.

He offered no defense. His parents offered no pardon.

Forty-five minutes later I asked his parents to give Justin and me some time together. They took a recess while I took a look below the waterline. Looking beyond Justin's behavior, I caught a glimpse of his beliefs. Although his parents were unaware that Justin was listening, at age nine he had overheard his parents arguing in their bedroom. The door had been left ajar. He remembered the conversation clearly, word for word. He described their dialogue in detail.

Late that night he discovered that he was the fourth child— in a family intended for three.

That night he crossed the line from being a child that had made a mistake to being a child that *was* a mistake. Justin's transformation didn't take long. Within months, his behaviors followed his beliefs, and his parents weren't able to connect the dots.

Houston, the problem is worse than we thought!

The messages that tell us we aren't worth much can come in many forms. Before kindergarten, we were compared to our siblings. During kindergarten, we were compared to our peers. Throughout elementary school, we were compared to our classmates. In high school, we took standardized tests and were compared to everyone our age—throughout North America! After graduation, men are judged by the size of their paychecks, and women are constantly compared to one another and are judged by the size of their waistlines.

More than ten years ago, an article in *USA Today* documented the need for and growth of programs in the public educational system that focused on building self-worth. Author Karen Peterson noted that in a survey of over one thousand teachers, 73 percent agreed that instilling self-worth "is the one aspect of teaching that is most important to helping students learn." As a result, programs were established in California, Florida, Hawaii, Kentucky, Louisiana, Maryland, New York, Ohio, and West Virginia, to name a few.[2]

Many of us struggle with our desire for perfection and peak performance, yet secretly long for permission to be accepted for who we are. At school, at work, and at home, we push ourselves to become world-class, but are often left feeling more like second-class. We long for someone to believe in us—even when we don't believe in ourselves.

Maybe Someone Does

Secretly you long to be a woman named Dulcinea, but truthfully you feel more like a woman named Aldonza.

Let me tell you the story.

In the Broadway musical "The Man of La Mancha," the grand idealist Don Quixote meets a harlot named Aldonza. From the moment he sees her, he notices something special about her and announces, "You will be my lady." To her shock and amazement, he adds, "Yes, you will be my lady and today I give you a new name. From now on, you will be called Dulcinea." Undaunted, Quixote believes in *her,* continues to affirm *her,* and declares to her not what she sees, but what he believes her to be.

The self-fulfilling prophecy will be tested once again.

The play continues, the dimly lit stage empty. Offstage a woman screams. It is Aldonza. She has been battered, abused, and raped. She appears onstage. Her blouse is torn, her face is covered with dirt, her eyes are full of fear, and it is evident that her heart is full of torment.

His voice shaking, Don Quixote says, "My lady, how could they do this to my lady?" But Aldonza feels dirty, degraded, disgraced, and discarded. Because she can't handle his admiration, she responds, "Don't call me your lady. I was born in a ditch by a mother who left me there naked, too cold to shiver, and too hungry to cry." With tears in her eyes and dust on her cheeks, she says, "Don't call me your lady.

I'm only a kitchen hand. I don't deserve to be your lady. My name is Aldonza." She disappears offstage. Quixote, the eternal optimist, shouts, "But you are my lady. You are my Dulcinea."

The curtain falls, but shortly thereafter it rises again to the death scene of the glorious dreamer. Don Quixote is now dying—dying more from a broken heart than from broken bones. He was ridiculed, rejected, and resented.

Suddenly to his side comes what appears to be a Spanish queen. As she kneels by him, he opens his eyes. Quixote asks, "Who are you?" She rises slowly. She stands tall. She stands proud. She has been transformed.

She responds, "Don't you remember? You called me your lady. You gave me a new name. My name is Dulcinea." The conversion is now complete. Her life will never be the same. Her future is limitless.[3]

That's why we believe in:

> ## PRINCIPLE #5:
> *Believe in Your Kids—*
> *Even When They Don't Believe in Themselves.*

Beauty will fade, bronze will fail, and brains will falter, but this one parenting principle will make a significant difference in the future of your child—regardless of her circumstances.

There's just one catch:
Believing in yourself is the beginning of believing in them.

Just as we've said before, you can't teach what you don't know, and you can't pass on what you don't have. Parents can't communicate that they believe in their kids if their kids get the feeling that their parents don't even believe in themselves.

Good point.

Maybe you're saying, "It's not that easy. Snow White became a princess because her father was her king. Aldonza stood tall as a Spanish queen because Don Quixote was her dreamer. But I'm no king and I'm no Quixote. What chance do my kids have of becoming princes or princesses if their parents are paupers?"

Good question.

Your child has a chance to become a princess as long as she's parented by parents...who are parented by Royalty. By a heavenly Father who can make an average parent into an awesome parent, a normal parent into a noble parent. This Father is the parent who owns the cattle on a thousand hills. A parent of unconditional love and unending grace. A parent who believes in His kids even when they don't believe in themselves.

Know anyone who fits this description? I do.

I know a King who has your name written on His heart. He is an eternal optimist. Just as Don Quixote believed in Aldonza, this divine King believes in you even when you don't believe in yourself. He stumbled upon a woman possessed with seven demons (an Aldonza). Scripture records that He healed her. That He transformed her. Her name? Mary Magdalene (see Luke 8:2). He believed in her and He trusted her. As a matter of fact, Mary Magdalene was the first to see Jesus risen, and she was the one He asked to tell the others of His resurrection (see John 20:11–18).

> *This King sees you as the one you can be*
> *instead of as the one you may be.*

God says, "For I know the thoughts that I think toward you, says the LORD, thoughts of peace and not of evil, to give you a future and a hope" (Jeremiah 29:11). After all, if God thinks so much of us that He sent His Son to save us, His Spirit to guide us, His Scripture to teach us, and His angels to guard us, something tells me that He values us even if we don't value ourselves.

Just how valuable are we to God? Valuable enough for Him to voluntarily give His life for us so that we could live with Him forever. If God thinks that much of us, then why can't we?

Why is it critical for parents to have a healthy sense of personal self-worth? Because it's unlikely that we'll ever handle others more effectively than how we handle ourselves. We become what we believe. We parent as we presume. It's unlikely that we'll build a sense of worth in others when it's lacking in us. After all, if we don't believe that we're valuable, why should our kids?

Self-worth: It's crucial to have and it's critical to impart. It's the key that can take unknown, unpopular, and underdeveloped kids and turn them into King's kids, who:

- develop high expectations for themselves,
- desire high expectations for their spouses,
- dream high expectations for their kids.

Jenni's Tips from the Trenches... to Turn Things Around

1. Encouragement is the fuel for a healthy sense of self-worth.

Self-worth can be built anytime and anywhere. Encouragement is the most effective tool for building it. In order to build a child's sense of self-worth, a parent must look for every opportunity to recognize internal character qualities such as courage, honesty, fairness, compassion, perseverance, and kindness.

Our friend Dr. Kevin Leman, a frequent guest on the program, is a down-to-earth psychologist who offers our viewers proven solutions to tough parental problems. Kevin believes that when you encourage your children, you help them feel that they are *accepted,* that they *belong,* and that they are *capable*—the ABCs of self-worth.[4]

Furthermore, he believes that although encouragement is helpful, praise is harmful. The difference? *Encouragement* focuses on a child's behavior and your appreciation of it. *Praise* focuses on a child's behavior and his or her value because of it. Need an example?

Encouragement: "I noticed that you cleaned your room this morning, and I just wanted to tell you that I really appreciate your helping me keep the house clean."

Praise: "You're really a great kid. I really love it when you clean your room and help me keep the house clean."

The difference between the two is subtle but significant. Encouragement is usually couched in "I" messages and focuses on performance without placing a value judgment on the performer. Praise is usually couched in "you" messages and focuses on the value of the performer because of the performance. One states that children are valuable because they did something, but the other one states that you're grateful something was done and you appreciate their effort.

If you encourage your kids more and praise them less, you just might hear your kids repeat the words of an eight-year-old boy who said, "I may not be perfect, but I am awesome!"[5]

2. Demonstrate unconditional love.

While encouragement may be the most important tool a parent can use to *instill* self-worth, unconditional love is the most important means of establishing a *feeling* of self-worth in your kids. *Unconditional* means that a child is loved "as is." This type of love is not dependent on "when" or "if" or anything else. When your children receive unconditional love, they develop a deep sense of confidence, security, and reassurance, which their mistakes cannot erase.

Verbally and behaviorally, parents can demonstrate unconditional love through an unexpected hug, a smile from across the room, a pat on the back, a small gift, or a quick "I love you."

Although there's no bad time to show your kids unconditional love, there is a best time to show it. When? Right after they spill their milk, right after they fail a test, right after they lose their textbook—for the fourth time! Personally, I've discovered that these are the times when I need to be loved the most—and the times when God seems to show up the most.

3. Avoid comparisons.

Making comparisons is great for window shopping, produce selecting, or automobile trading. But comparing your kids with others will leave them feeling depressed and discouraged. Negative comparisons such as "You should save your allowance like your sister Judy. She had enough money to buy a watch last year and didn't have to ask us for money to go to the movies" are deflating. Just as bad are positive comparisons like "It's sure nice that you cleaned up your room. Your brother Tyler is such a slob. You'd think he was born in a barn!" The first comparison leaves a person feeling resentful, the second self-righteous.

Comparisons will inevitably lead to increased sibling rivalry and excessive peer competition. Both are destructive to social and family life. Both are detrimental to a child's sense of self-worth. It's natural for parents to notice diversity among their children but appreciate the differences, value individuality, and avoid comparisons.

4. Separate the incident from the individual.

Dumb, slow, gifted, shy, funny, crybaby, smarty-pants—no matter what the label, they are hard to undo and harder to outlive. Labeling is commonly done by both peers and parents. But whether positive or negative, labels are confining, discouraging, and often self-fulfilling. At minimum, labels influence how others think about children, and they unfortunately influence how children think about themselves. When we believe a label, we become the label. Even common terms like the "terrible twos" or the "rebellious teens" are dangerous and set the parameters for expected behavior.

Positive labels also have consequences. Will a girl labeled as "gifted" not feel discouraged with an average grade? Will a boy labeled as a "jock" pursue art or music? Will "daddy's girl" ever have a special relationship with her mom? If we have carelessly labeled our children, then we must carefully teach them to overcome those labels.

Furthermore, when it comes to discipline, we must be

careful not to connect person to performance. Our words can become permanently embedded in a child's mind when spilled milk elicits a response like, "You're so clumsy," or when a failed test results in a remark like, "You're so dumb," or when missing the bus nets an insult like, "Well, here comes Johnny-come-lately." Kids as well as adults are more than *incidents*—even if the incident is repeated. There's a big difference between someone who *made a mistake* and someone who *is a mistake*, between someone who *told a lie* and someone who *is a liar*.

When you respond to inappropriate behavior, separate the incident from the individual. You can do this with statements like, "Ryan, your mother and I are disappointed to hear that you took Lisa's bike at school. I know you know better than that because I've seen you respect other people's property before." This statement challenges his behavior while encouraging his identity. Ryan's not a thief. He did take a bike that was not his. He must apologize and face the consequences. But it is important to emphasize the fact that although Ryan made a mistake, we don't believe that Ryan is a mistake.

5. Recognize effort and celebrate progress.

From the classroom to the corporate boardroom, we live in a results-oriented society. Because of that, personal effort takes a backseat to personal performance. Unfortunately, much of the time class grades are compared while personal progress is ignored. The system focuses on success, not progress. No wonder the concept of "winning at all costs" has become commonplace for our kids. This was evidenced in the 2001 Little League World Series, when a pitcher playing for the winning team from New York City was found to be two years over the twelve-year-old age limit and the team had to forfeit the championship.

Principle-centered parents who want to build character and develop their children's sense of self-worth will focus on effort rather than on outcome, on progress rather than on performance. They'll acknowledge effort in the classroom, on the court, and in the choir—regardless of outcome. That means that a test taken in school is a lesson learned (not just a grade). A game played on the court is an experience gained (not just a score). A song sung in church is a worship opportunity (not just a chance for a compliment).

6. Avoid reliving past failures.

Somewhere, parents got the impression that kids who have made mistakes also have a memory disorder and need constant reminding in order not to repeat them. Nothing can be more demoralizing to kids than to constantly wear a "mark of failure" on their foreheads.

Instead, focus on a child's strength, without mentioning past failures. Comments like, "You did it! See what you can do when you really try?" should be reworded so that they are not actually backhanded compliments. A better approach might be, "You did it! You tried and tried and never gave up. I knew you could do it." Another misguided assessment might be, "Your room looks great. I can't see any of the dirty clothes you left on your bed yesterday." It could be better expressed with something like, "Your room looks great! I think you'll really enjoy a clean room, and I really appreciate how you're helping to keep our house clean."

Believe in your children and they'll believe in themselves.
God believes in you. Your kids need you to believe in them.

Chapter Six

WHEN THE MASKS WE WEAR...MAKE IT HARD TO BE "TRANS-PARENT"

Choosing to Be Real over Craving to Be Perfect.

This above all: to thine own self be true.

WILLIAM SHAKESPEARE

By the time you're Real, most of your hair has been loved off....
But these things don't matter at all, because once you are
Real you can't be ugly, except to people who don't understand.

MARGERY WILLIAMS, *THE VELVETEEN RABBIT*

LET'S TALK WITH JENNI

I WAS FLAPPING MY ARMS AS FAST as I could. And going nowhere! With my head held high and my chest pushed forward, I flapped some more, adding the majestic stride of a gold medal skater. Gliding and flapping. Gliding and flapping. I circled, looking for some kind of response—any kind of response.

Nothing. I took a deep breath. I gave it one last try. This time I wrinkled my face, contorted my arms, and hunched over. I looked as unsightly as possible (which doesn't come naturally!). Then, slowly, a caterpillar became a butterfly. I relaxed my face, held my head high, and flapped my arms while gliding gracefully around the room. It was perfection. Baryshnikov could do no better. It was poetry in motion. Flap and glide. Flap and glide. Flap and…

"Time!"

My flight was interrupted. My teenage daughter Brittany announced that my time was up. I growled. I grunted. I snapped at my partner, "What's wrong with you? You didn't get it? How could you not get it! It was obvious to everyone." (It was obvious to me that my partner had a cognitive disability!)

"I was the ugly duckling turning into a graceful swan! How could you not see the obvious?"

My criticism was surprising to my partner and revealing to me. It was only a game. A friendly game of charades—mothers versus daughters. And I was acting like it was the World Series of recreation, the Super Bowl of entertainment.

What's the big deal?
Why the frustration?
What's the problem?

We were losing—to our daughters! Correction, not just losing— it wasn't even close—we were barely on the field. It was like a defenseless Christian being fed to the lions. Despite my Emmy Award–winning performances, we didn't get a single answer right all night. It was unbelievable! And to top it off, my daughter and her best friend sat smugly across the room. They were gloating. They were glaring. They were heartless. It was unmerciful.

Family tradition dictated that the losers make the victors a super-duper ice cream sundae. So my partner and I trudged to the kitchen. The girls thought we went to the kitchen to make their treat, but it was more a retreat so that we could lick our wounds.

Later that evening the torture continued, not in the family room but in my head. I couldn't get the events of our game off my mind. I began to think about how amazing it was to watch my daughter and her friend act out and guess each charade. They had similarity of thought and symmetry of spirit. These fourteen-year-old girls knew each other so well that they never needed more than a few clues. They just seemed to know—without saying a word.

Later that night when I was tucking Brittany into bed, I asked her about her friendship with Andrea. I asked her how she knew what Andrea was thinking. How they seemed to read each other's minds. How they were able to communicate so well after being friends for only three short years. How?

Brittany was blunt. "We're honest with each other. We talk. We argue. We disagree. But underneath it all, I think it's that we're honest with each other. We don't have to watch what we say or worry about what we think. We're friends."

That was bad enough.... Then came the knife to the heart, the bamboo under the fingertips, the mother lode of all indictments, the final blow.

"Andrea and I have decided to be honest rather than to be perfect. You oughta try it," Brittany said.

My spirit was crippled. My feelings were crushed.
My heart fell to the floor.

I left Brittany's room that night wondering how a fourteen-year-old could be so much farther down the relational road than her forty-something mother. What a strange feeling it is to have your daughter teach you such a profound truth about relationships. I began to think about all my relationships and the "Jenni" I worked so hard to perfect…and to project. Clairol for my hair, Revlon for my cheeks, Wonder for my…never mind, you get the idea. Then I wondered how many people in my life know the "real" me anyhow.

And do I?

Just like many of you, I have lived my life from behind a mask. The man-made mask of pretend: the perfect Christian, the supportive wife, the dedicated mother, the forgiving friend, the Proverbs 31 woman. As I smiled my way through life, I had become an actor playing a role, dressed in someone else's skin. A chameleon. I carried my burdens alone. I buried them deep within my heart, where they rarely saw the light of day. They surfaced only at night…when I was alone…when I was safe.

Then I realized that I was modeling this behavior to my kids.

That night I decided to take it off. Take it all off. I began the task of peeling away the layers of my self-imposed shell of pretend and perfection. I determined that I want to be real—to share with those around me my hurts, my failures, and my dreams. To reveal the real me and to accept the one I found.

But then came the question, "So who am I?"

I'd like to tell you that I found the answer to that question and that I now live my life in the land of real. But to be honest, it's something I struggle with every day.

With each new sunrise comes the temptation to hide behind the mask. On most days I resist and decide it's better to be the real me than it is to be someone else, anyone else—even if she does appear to be perfect. I've discovered that being real is scary, but being authentic is better than being artificial. When I succeed, I feel great. When I fail, I feel like a fraud. But a good friend once revealed to me the truth behind the saying, "I'm not okay, and you're not okay—but that's okay."

LET'S TALK WITH CHUCK

Jenni's words remind me of another "pretender," who penned the following words. The feelings are real. They could have been mine:

Please Hear What I'm Not Saying

Don't be fooled by me.
Don't be fooled by the mask I wear
for I wear a thousand masks,
masks that I'm afraid to take off,
and none of them is the real me.

Pretending is an art that's second nature to me,
but don't be fooled.
I give you the impression that I'm secure,
that all is sunny and unruffled with me, within as well as without,
that confidence is my name and coolness my game.

I tell you everything that's really nothing,
and nothing of what's everything,
of what's crying within me.
So when I'm going through my routine
don't be fooled by what I'm saying.
Please listen carefully and try to hear what I'm not saying.

Only you can call me into aliveness.
Each time you're kind, and gentle, and encouraging,
each time you try to understand because you really care,
my heart begins to grow wings—
very small wings,
very feeble wings,
but wings!

You alone can break down the wall behind which I tremble,
you alone can remove my mask,
you alone can release me from my shadow-world of panic,
from my lonely prison,
if you choose to.
Please choose to.

I fight against the very thing I cry out for.
But I am told that love is stronger than strong walls
and in this lies my hope.

Please try to beat down those walls
with firm hands but gentle hands
for a child is very sensitive.

Who am I you may wonder?
I am someone you know very well.
For I am every man you meet
and I am every woman you meet. [1]

CHARLIE FINN

Sound familiar? It should. It was written by every one of us who prefers to present an image rather than an individual. Just like the Shunammite woman in 2 Kings 4:8–37.

Although never mentioned by name, the Shunammite woman is described as a "notable" woman, an elderly woman who lived with her husband in the town of Shunem, a village in southern Galilee. Her home had become a frequent stopover for the prophet Elisha during his journeys throughout the countryside. Her hospitality was praiseworthy, as she went so far as to build a place for this prophet: a small upper room with a bed, table, chair, and lampstand (see v. 10).

In return, Elisha announced that the Shunammite woman's infertility would end within a year. His prophecy came true, but this mother's happiness soon turned to heartache.

Elisha was on the road, her husband was working in the fields, and the Shunammite woman was cradling her child on her lap…when he died. She laid her son's corpse on the bed in the upper room, Elisha's room. Then she summoned for a servant and a donkey and set out on a journey to Mt. Carmel to find Elisha. When asked by her husband about the haste for her trip, she replied, "It is well."

Grieving the loss of her only child, she responded to her uninformed husband, "It is well." This was no stranger she was responding to; he was the husband she loved, the husband she knew best, the father of this lifeless child.

Was this accurate?
Was this authentic?
Was this appropriate?

Don't be fooled by the mask I wear.

From a distance, Elisha recognized the Shunammite woman as she drew near. Like her husband, Elisha was unaware of her loss. He instructed his servant to run to her and inquire, "How are you doing? How is your husband? How is your son?" Once again her response was, "It is well."

For I wear a thousand masks…and none of them is the real me.

Was she diplomatic or dishonest?
Authentic or artificial?
Factual or forgetful?
Was she a woman of faith or just another phony Pharisee?

Just like when Jesus confronted the woman at the well, Elisha could see past the Shunammite woman's tale and sense her torment. He looked to the condition of her heart rather than at the content of her words. Something was wrong.

Finally, the Shunammite woman came clean. She fell at the feet of this holy man and declared, "My son is dead." Like any desperate parent would, she requested the prayers of a prophet and wouldn't relent until he returned with her. Sure enough, lying on Elisha's bed was the boy—the gift from God now gone. Elisha prayed and then lay upon the boy—mouth to mouth, eyes to eyes, and hands to hands. Not once but twice. A miracle occurred and a new dawn was given to the deceased. He was alive. Again.

The Shunammite woman fell at the feet of this miracle man once again, this time from gratitude rather than from gloom. A mother had her child to hold by her heart. A father had his son to continue his heritage. A family experienced a miracle to strengthen their faith.

But why the dance of deception? Why the dishonesty?
Why the charade?

Rather than ask this Shunammite why she wasn't more straightforward, maybe we need to ask ourselves why *we're* not more forthcoming, more candid, and more truthful in our own lives. Why aren't we more "real" and less restrained? Why aren't we more authentic and less artificial? Think about the times when...

- a coworker asked how you were doing and you said "fine." Yet you failed to mention that you were placed on probation yesterday and were on the verge of falling apart emotionally.
- a friend asked why you were late for lunch and you said "traffic," yet failed to mention that the bank called because you were overdue on your mortgage. Again.
- your son's teacher at school noticed his grades falling and asked why. You said, "He needs more sleep," yet failed to mention that he also needed his father to

return home. He left eight weeks ago.

- your pastor hadn't seen you all summer and asked where you'd been. You replied, "Oh, here and there," yet failed to add that you were admitted to St. Joseph's Hospital. Psychiatric unit.
- your church's youth pastor asked you how things were going at home and you said "great," yet failed to mention that you and your teenage son hadn't spoken in weeks.
- you went to church and arrived conveniently late with a smile on your face and new shoes on your feet to hide the fact that you had filed for bankruptcy last Friday.
- the tests came back positive...
- the diet became a disorder...
- the...

Do I need to continue?

These are all classic examples of how the person on the inside fails to resemble the person on the outside.

Opportunities to reveal the real you prevail but the loneliness persists. People at the office. People at church. People at the fitness center. People everywhere, yet nobody knows the real you.

Not your spouse. Not your best friend.
Not your kids. Not even you.

We talk but say little. We discuss everything from the state of the union to the state of the stock market—all to avoid revealing the state of our hearts or the condition of our homes. We fill space with words but say nothing that really matters; we talk about everything that means nothing.

We're not alone.... Robert Redford was once spotted in a hotel lobby by a devoted fan. Just as Redford stepped into the elevator and waited for the door to close, the opportunistic fan took the chance to confirm Redford's identity. She asked, "Are you the *real* Robert Redford?" Redford paused and then responded, "Only when I'm alone." The elevator door closed.

Most of us are a combination of "the me I really am," "the me I pretend to be," and "the me I long to be." So there I am, just the three of me! Our kids are looking for parents to be a stabilizing force in an ever changing world, but find themselves wondering which of their "three parents" are coming home from the office today.

That's why we believe in:

> ## PRINCIPLE #6:
> *Choosing to be Real over Craving to Be Perfect.*

Becoming "Trans-Parent"

Lee Ezell, a gifted author whom we've interviewed on the program many times, calls living a transparent life "see-through Christianity." She defines a transparent person as one who is:

- guileless in life,
- frank about feelings,
- open about issues of the heart,
- easily detected—obvious in motive and readily understood,
- honest in behavior, unpretentious in conduct, and approachable in all settings.[2]

Doesn't that sound like the kind of parent you want to be? One that your kids will trust? Doesn't that sound like the kind of spouse you long to be? One that your mate will believe? Doesn't that sound like the kind of friend you hope to be? One that will be honest, genuine, and sincere?

But how does an artificial person become an authentic person? How does a tentative parent become "trans-parent"? What books should I read? What seminars should I attend? What teachers should I seek out? Who knows the process for becoming trans-parent?

The Skin Horse Knows

One Christmas morning, a Velveteen Rabbit, unblemished and unloved, sat with eager expectation inside a little boy's Christmas stocking. The boy was delighted with his new toy, but only for an hour or two. Replaced by other toys, the stuffed rabbit was placed on the shelf beside the Skin Horse. Here he became aware of the emptiness of his spirit and the hollowness of his heart. The journey had begun.

One day, the Rabbit asked the worn but insightful Skin Horse, "What is REAL?" The weathered warrior of the nursery, who had seen many toys come and go during his years, replied, "Real isn't how you are made. It's a thing that happens to you. When a child loves you for a long, long time, not just to play with, but REALLY loves you, then you become Real."

So far so good, but there must be a catch.

"Does it hurt?" asked the Rabbit.

"Sometimes," said the Skin Horse, for he was always truthful. "When you are Real you don't mind being hurt."

This sounds like theological double-talk.
You know, the least becomes the greatest, the last will be first,
he who loses his life finds it.

"Does it happen all at once, like being wound up," he asked, "or bit by bit?"

"It doesn't happen all at once," said the Skin Horse. "You become. It takes a long time. That's why it doesn't happen often to people who break easily, or have sharp edges, or who have to be carefully kept. Generally, by the time you are Real, most of your hair has been loved off, and your eyes drop out and you get loose in your joints and very shabby. But these things don't matter at all, because once you are Real you can't be ugly, except to people who don't understand."[3]

Double-talk or not, sign me up.
God is looking for us to be "authentic."
And our kids are looking for us to be "trans-parent."
So what about you?

Maybe you've hopped along rabbit trails and noticed many detours and dead ends. Perhaps you've stood at that famous fork in the road that left you paralyzed. One path leads to the Land of Pretend while the path less traveled leads to the Land of Real. Just as you feared, it will be the tough and trying road that will transform you from artificial to authentic—an authentic parent your kids can connect with.

But the road less traveled has its rewards. The more real you become, the more meaningful your relationships will be. And the more real you become, the more you will inspire your family to travel from the Land of Pretend to the Land of Real.

The Land of Pretend	The Land of Real
Artificial	Authentic
Religious	Spiritual
Invincible	Vulnerable
Self-Sufficient	Others-Reliant
Independent	Interdependent
Values Things	Values People
Fact Based	Faith Based
Secure	Scared
Busy	Effective
Superficial	Substantial

With our fears, our faults, and our failures exposed, we are able to give up our pat answers and our notion that we have a solution for every struggle. We can now live in the world of the honest, the sincere, and the "trans-parent."

Not spotless, but sincere.
Not guarded, but growing.
Not shrewd, but straightforward.

For those of us who are tempted to remain in the Land of Pretend, we have to ask ourselves, "Why?" Many of us stay because of a fear of rejection. A fear that real might not be good enough. *What if real is rejected? Then I'll have nowhere to turn, nowhere to hide, and no one to blame. What if the real me is not enough to be loved, not enough to be accepted, or not enough to par-*

ent? In all honesty, most of us would rather pretend than discover that we're not enough, and if that were the inevitable conclusion, I would have to agree with this argument. But I don't think it is.

Take it from a parent who's constantly learning and from a professional who's constantly counseling. I have concluded that the best I have to offer my friends, my family, and my heavenly Father is to be an *authentic me* rather than an *artificial me.* God never asked us to be perfect, but to be principled. He never expected us to be sinless, but to be sincere (see Luke 18:10–14). So why should I try to be anything less (or more) for my family and friends?

Now for those who continue to remain in the Land of Pretend because you realize that the journey to the Land of Real will be difficult and the process will be demanding, I have a question for you: *If you can't be you now, when can you be?*

> *You're the only one who can be you and get it right.*
> LEE EZELL

And for those who are concerned about the cost of conversion from artificial to authentic, I have another question for you: *If you have to give up the* real *you in order to be loved or accepted by someone else, isn't that an awfully expensive price tag?*

This conversion isn't just costly; it's priceless.

> *The best thing my dad gave me was a glimpse of his faults.*
> DR. PAUL FAULKNER

Isn't *real* what our kids really want?
Isn't *real* what our kids really need?
Isn't *real* what you want your kids to become?

Although our world constantly bombards us with messages that steer us toward a designer identity, let me encourage you to look in the "parental lost and found" to find the *real* you:

- with your hair loved off,
- your eyes dropped out,
- and all loose in your joints.

Your kids will never let you go!

Authentic living for parents is critical.
Because while parents may play an important part
in the lives of their kids,
in their own life, they play the principal part.

Jenni's Tips from the Trenches… to Turn Things Around

1.   Admit we're artificial and begin living from the inside out.

Okay, I admit it…I'm not the mom you might think I am. Real moms have fresh cookies and cold milk waiting for their kids after school. They volunteer for the science fair at school and in the nursery at church. On the other hand, I work outside the home. My schedule is a little more complicated. Sometimes I bring home doughnuts—but they're usually leftovers from the office. I'm too busy *making* my kid's science project to volunteer for an administrative job at the fair, and Sunday *has* been declared an official day of rest!

Okay, so I'm not the woman you think I am either. I talk about being "real"—with highlighted hair, contact lenses, Bobbi Brown makeup, ten acrylic nails, two capped teeth, and support hose! Are you sure you're ready for *real?*

And worse than that…on the inside, I'm not the person you think I am either. Inside, I'm not nearly as confident as I pretend. I laugh when I'm nervous. I'm silent when I'm scared. There have been times in my life when I've felt depressed, disappointed, angry, fearful, insecure, and inadequate. Times when I've felt as though I had more questions than answers. I've felt the pressure of living in a glass house, and I've tried to soar like an eagle when the world was weighing me down. I will say this though: The more I tried to hide, the farther I felt from home.

I've discovered that the solution is not to outrun your feelings, but to own them. You'll never be able to run fast enough, so you're left with the choice to either go public or stay plastic. I remember sitting with Sandi Patty as she talked about her extramarital affair, divorce, and remarriage. In the midst of her travail, she discovered a truth hidden in Scripture that changed her life. She discovered the power behind Jesus' words: "You shall know the truth, and the truth shall make you free" (John 8:32). Previously, she had lived a lie and the lie had kept her in bondage. Instead of trying to keep her secrets hidden, she found great freedom in authentic living. Now she talks freely about her faults and failures—and travels *free*.

Lee Ezell developed an exercise that invites us to strip away the layers of designer clothing and image consultants and become real. If you're ready to exchange artificial for authentic, plastic for pure, try this:

Certificate of Authenticity
    Permission is hereby granted for __(your name)__ to be *herself* (or *himself*). I permit myself to risk expressing my genuine feelings and opinions, to communicate

the real me in all its originality, without appearing to fit in or blend in with the crowd. I permit myself to become the person that God intended me to be, without fear, without apology, without wearing a mask or dishonest disguises.

Signed: _____

Date: _____

No one can go back and start over, but everyone can begin today to create a new tomorrow.

2.   Apologize for not being real.

To my spouse: I'm sorry for failing to be real and hindering intimacy in the process.

To my friends: I'm sorry for hiding behind the masks I've worn for fear you wouldn't like who you saw.

To my kids: I'm sorry for letting *me* get in the way of being the mommy you deserve.

To my coworkers: I'm sorry for hiding behind my title.

To God: I'm sorry for taking so long to accept myself and become the person You designed me to be.

To myself: I'm sorry it took so long to listen to the words of a Skin Horse.

3.   Model it—be real.

There is no greater teacher for your kids than the modeling you provide every day within your home. Parents continue to remain at the top of the list when it comes to the people who have made the greatest impact on children's lives.

So once you've become real, let your kids see it. Let them see that you are transparent about your successes *and* your shortcomings. Begin conversations with, "Boy, did I ever blow it today." It will not be our flawlessness that draws people to us, but our faults. Not our medals, but our mistakes. Be real. Model real.

> *Example is not the main thing in influencing others.*
> *It is the only thing.*
> ALBERT SCHWEITZER

4. Answer truthfully, not just tactfully.

You can be assured that within the first thirteen years of their lives, your kids will ask you every single question you *don't* have an answer for! Questions on everything from sex to the Savior. If they haven't asked yet, they will.

Early on, we experienced an ever present parent trap. This occurs when your kids look at you and say "Gotcha!" with their eyes. The issue centered on old Saint Nick—that's right, Santa Claus. When the inevitable question of his reality arose, we tactfully went with the flow and did the "he lives at the North Pole" thing. (Hey, we didn't want to be the grinch who stole Christmas!) As our kids got older and the likelihood of Santa's existence grew dim, we simply let the kids discover the truth on their own.

Well, sure enough, when Brittany was in first grade, her friend Derrick spilled the beans—and she was mortified! She came home and told us that Derrick was telling lies about Santa Claus and that she knew Santa was real because we had told her so. Now we were mortified!

It was then that we decided that it's never okay to tell your kids one thing today—whether it's about the Easter Bunny, the Tooth Fairy, or Santa Claus—only to tell them something different tomorrow. If you do, they will be left wondering when to believe you and when not to. Fairy tales are one thing, but faith in God is another. If your kids don't know when they can believe you, they will inevitably question your faith as well as your fables.

That doesn't mean we're committed to taking the fun or the fantasy out of make-believe. But when our kids asked, we found it better to tell them something like "You know, many kids your age believe in Santa and we don't want to ruin it for them, but the truth is that many years ago a man named Saint Nicholas lived and did many wonderful things for the kids in his neighborhood. But because he lived so long ago, now it's up to mommies and daddies to fill in for him."

Trust is a sacred gem. Why sacrifice it over the Tooth Fairy?

5. Live in the here and now.

Parents who spend more time living in the present (the here and now) are more likely to be in touch with their own thoughts and feelings. They tend to see issues more clearly and deal with them more effectively because they're not reliving their past or fearing their future. Each marital and parental challenge is addressed independently, without being influenced by what happened yesterday or what might happen tomorrow. In general, living in the present allows people to *feel* in the present, unclouded by leftover emotions.

Teach your kids how to seize each moment and live it to

the fullest. Teach them how to live now, love now, and be real now. Teach them how to express their feelings in the present tense, beginning sentences with, "I feel…" Teach them to express their thoughts, beginning sentences with, "I think…" And teach them how to let go of the way of the world and prefer the way of the Word. "And do not be conformed to this world, but be transformed by the renewing of your mind" (Romans 12:2).

Wanna know yourself, like yourself, and be yourself?
Then live life in the here and now.

6. Reduce role-playing.

Real is not a role. We live in an artificial world, so "real" parents must also let go of their tendencies to wrap their kids in a role. Scripture instructs parents to "train up a child in the way *he* should go" (Proverbs 22:6, emphasis added), not in the way *his parents* want him to go. Not in the way his parents wish they had gone. And not in the way the world wants him to go.

Whether you're a birth parent, stepparent, adoptive parent, or foster parent, I'm sure you're well aware of the individual traits and talents of each of your children. As parents, we need to discover and develop our kids' talents rather than dictate them.

Our children's futures should be defined by God's design and their dreams, rather than by our demands or desires.

Finally, we're convinced that:

- with more truth and less tact,
- with more fiber and less filler,

- with more dignity and less deception,
- with more character and less cunning,
- with more decency and less diplomacy,
- with one more "I love you" and one less "you need to,"
- we will teach our kids how to be authentic in a world that's largely artificial.

Chapter Seven

WHEN THE KIDS ARE PULLING YOU APART...AND YOU'RE DETERMINED TO STICK TOGETHER

Choose Marriage over Minors and

"Couplehood" over Parenthood.

The thing that impresses me most about America is the way parents obey their children.

EDWARD VIII, DUKE OF WINDSOR

The latest research concludes that insanity is hereditary. Parents get it from their kids.

UNKNOWN

LET'S TALK WITH JENNI

I PULLED INTO THE PARKING LOT and checked my watch. I had 3.5 minutes to get the cupcakes to Room 204 for Cody's "Spring Has Sprung" homeroom party.

No problem. I can do this. I gave birth to this boy—a whopping ten pounds, four ounces—I can deliver the goods!

I reached into the backseat and lifted the foil to make sure that none of my creations had been smushed, smashed, or smudged (and yes, there is a difference). And there they were—twenty-seven flawless cupcakes.

Perfection feels noble even if it does have a price tag. I concluded that it was well worth the drive to three different stores to find the "super sprinkles" and the extra trip to the grocery store to pick up the bright blue foil wrappers instead of settling for the lifeless pastel paper wrappers.

As I looked at the cupcakes, I had a "Martha Stewart" moment. I thought to myself, *Move over, Martha. I am Mother of the Year material!* In fact, I would even go so far as to say that I was thinking I had surpassed Wonder Woman and had entered the distinctive domain of Supermom! I could just picture Cody and his classmates *oohing* and *aahing* as I unwrapped each of my priceless creations. In my mind I could hear their praises echoing like the Brooklyn Tabernacle Choir, "Oh, Mrs. Borsellino. You are the *best* mom in the whole world! Cody is soooooooo lucky. These are the coolest cupcakes we have ever seen."

I yawned as I checked my watch again. Staying up until midnight to work on the cupcakes had left me tired, but my payoff was just around the corner. This had been one of those weeks. I'd been running nonstop all week long: football practice, gymnastics, basketball, piano, soccer. On top of that, homework, science projects, and spelling words needed my attention. Not to mention friends after school, a sleepover on Friday, and a birthday party over the weekend. Just to finish me off, Courtney had *"nothing"* to wear—so off to the mall we went!

Yes, it was exhausting, but I love my children. Just like you, I'd do anything for them. After all, that's what parenting is all about, right? Yawning again, I hopped out of the car, picked up the cupcakes, and headed down the school corridor. I arrived at Room 204 with cupcakes in hand, not a minute too soon. As I set the cupcakes down on the classroom table, I was overwhelmed—not by gratitude, but by grief!

In a matter of seconds, fifty-four grubby little paws were grabbing in unison for my perfect cupcakes. Not one of them took the time to recognize the works of art I had created. Instead, like a crowd of famished bear cubs, they grabbed my beautifully decorated marvels and gobbled them down faster than I could say "Hi, kids." It was a feeding frenzy! I watched in horror as the children devoured their cupcakes without a bit of gratitude or an ounce of appreciation.

I was speechless...and that doesn't happen very often!

My cupcakes were a hit, but my feelings were hurt and my heart was troubled. When I turned to leave, all I could think about was calling Chuck.

After the classroom door closed behind me, I listened for a few moments to the children's lighthearted laughter at the "Spring Has Sprung" event that now held their attention. I wondered if I had invested my time wisely. What about the super sprinkles that required the extra trip? What about the blue foil wrappers that said "I've gone the extra mile for you"?

Why did I feel so empty? Why did I feel so lifeless?

I wanted my best friend. I wanted Chuck to hold me and tell me they were just cupcakes. I wanted him to tell me how proud of me he was. I wanted him to tell me that even if the kids didn't recognize it, he thought I was Supermom and he appreciated the extra effort I had put into those glittering gourmet cupcakes. I imagined Chuck holding my face in his hands, looking into my eyes, and just staring at me as if he were memorizing my every facial feature. Then, at that moment, standing outside Room 204, I woke up—and realized that my priorities had been misdirected.

God has always been first on my priority list, but my children had inched up to second—and my spouse had dropped like a rock to a distant third. I asked myself, *When was the last time I spent this much time making something special for Chuck?*

I began to relive the past few days in my mind. Last Friday, Chuck had invited some friends over for the evening. They all wanted to fix pan-fried, home-cooked favorites; I ordered a pizza. On Saturday, he had planned for us to have Date Night with dinner and a movie; I had offered him a rain check so I could take Brittany and her friends to the mall. On Sunday afternoon, Chuck had wanted to go for a walk, but I had thought it best to start Cody's "Atoms in the Universe" project. One by one I remembered my decisions over the past few days, and although many of them might have qualified me for Supermom status, not one of them would suggest that I was interested in holding the title of Superspouse.

I had to ask myself some difficult questions. What kind of role model was I being for my daughters? Is this how I wanted them to treat their husbands? Did they notice when I pushed their dad aside? Did Chuck feel that I would be there for him—after the kids graduated and moved on?

Needless to say, that day my priorities began to change. I adore my kids. I love parenthood. But being a good parent is more than taxi-driving and cupcake-making. Oddly enough, this is one of the most neglected principles of good parenthood: *Strong and healthy couples usually raise strong and healthy kids.*

Children were designed to enrich a marriage.
Not replace it. Not divide it.

That night Chuck arrived home to a new home and a new wife. I had a neighbor take the kids to their practices. She had offered to do this a million times before, but I had always told myself that Supermoms do it themselves—all the time. But this night was different. Chuck and I sat at the dinner table and talked—just the two of us. I had not realized how much I missed him—my husband, my lover, my best friend. We got up from the table with a twinkle in our eyes. I knew what Chuck was thinking.

Words were unnecessary.
We had been there before.

There was a bounce to Chuck's step and a sparkle in my eyes. We knew what would come next. Chuck's going to kill me for telling you this, but I never have been able keep a secret. There we were—no commitments to keep, no homework to correct, and no kids in sight. You know what they say: "Seize the moment." So we did. We looked at each other...and then ate all the remaining cupcakes on the platter!

Let's Talk with Chuck:
The Dysfunction Junction

Jenni's not alone. I've been there too. As an aging athlete, I've been an FAA (Frustrated All-American) for some time now. Like many who went before me, I once had visions of NCAA college championships, Super Bowl rings, and MVP Trophies. Unfortunately, that's all they were: visions. But with kids, the door was still open. The dream was still alive.

First it was soccer. At practices and at games, I praised—then I pushed. First as a parent and then as a coach. Brittany was first, Cody came next, and Courtney was soon to follow. When Brittany became more interested in finding four-leaf clovers than guarding her goal, it was time for me to move on—to Cody and karate.

Yep, I was going to take him all the way. Cody had what it took: skill, strength, stamina, and superior genes! He also had a dad who said good-bye to his spouse when it came to daily practices, weekly lessons, and quarterly tournaments. The goal was a black belt. I paid the price with my time, and Jenni saw little of me until Cody stepped forward to receive his belt.

When Cody was awarded his black belt at age ten, Jenni and I looked at each other and asked, "Now what?" Modeling for Brittany, gymnastics for Courtney, football for Cody. But wait a minute. We can't leave out piano, baseball, voice lessons, tennis, golf, art classes, Young Life, cheerleading, Hooked on Phonics, and the chess club. There's always more. There's never an end—until we realize that we are sacrificing our relationship when we put minors before marriage.

Families were designed to be spouse-centered, not child-centered.

Something tells me we're not alone. Recently, our pastor was preparing to speak about parenthood and conducted his research at one of the most renowned parental pit stops: Starbucks. While he was there he overheard one young toddler-toting mom say to another, "You know, I think I'm a great mom. I just don't think I'm a very good wife." Unfortunately, many of us would have to admit that we've been *great parents,* but *poor partners.*

You might be wondering how you can tell if this parental shoe fits. Take this quiz:

Signs You Don't Have a Life Outside of Parenthood

1. T or F   You haven't been to a movie since *The Poseidon Adventure.*
2. T or F   Your kids are sleeping in your bed at night.
3. T or F   Your toddler sits with you in church rather than staying in the nursery.
4. T or F   Your largest monthly bill is from Toys "R" Us.
5. T or F   Your kids' success means more to you than it does to them.
6. T or F   Your home office is now a Nintendo headquarters.
7. T or F   Your school-age kids stay up later than you do.
8. T or F   Your life revolves around soccer, gymnastics, and piano lessons.
9. T or F   Your kids have custody of the remote control.
10. T or F   Your twenty-eight-year-old son won't leave home without you.

Scoring:

If you answered true to *any* of the above, you have a problem!

A Parent Is Born, a Marriage Is Broken

The situation they were in was unfortunate. It was unnecessary. It wasn't designed to be this way.

If you look around, you'll find these parents wherever you go. Maybe they sit beside you at church. Maybe they work next to you at the office. They look just like other caring, compassionate parents.

Maybe they look just like you.

If you can't quite identify them yet, let me introduce you to Larry and Beth, a couple focused on their kids—first Dillon, then Ashley. They had been married for four years when a beautiful baby boy arrived. Mom was delighted. Dad was delirious. Soon Dad had accumulated a garage full of sports equipment for his son: bikes, baseballs, in-line skates, hockey sticks, and golf clubs. Beth felt neglected, ignored, and replaced.

She used to enjoy long walks down the lane and naps under the willow tree with Larry. But now he's busy with other things. If it's not work, it's playtime with his prodigy. A marital crack develops. Their relationship begins taking on water. Beth shares her feelings with Larry. He minimizes them. He rationalizes them. He says it's only temporary. She's not convinced.

Soon Beth finds a solution—another child. The answer to her emotional hunger arrives on the scene soon thereafter. Beth takes great delight in shopping for frilly dresses and fancy bedroom furniture. Dad responds: He's gone fishing with his four-year-old son. The gap grows wider. Unknowingly, both of these parents have traded marriage for parenthood. They offer their kids every opportunity to succeed in school and in sports. Two to three extracurricular activities are scheduled for each child. Larry and Beth don't want their kids to miss out, to miss the activities that they never experienced.

To be truthful, placing their focus on their kids also provided an opportunity for Larry and Beth to avoid each other. Their marriage relationship cooled and they grew more and more distant. Their conversation centered on "the kids"—their schedules, their school supplies, and their sports selections for next season. While all appeared okay on the surface, below the surface the problem was evident:

Parents focused primarily on their children are parents focused minimally on their marriage.

Most of us saw Larry and Beth as warm, caring, attentive parents—and they were. However, attention on their kids gradually *replaced* attention on each other. It began first with Larry and then spilled over to Beth. Eventually, the kids became the glue in this couple's relationship. When their kids finished high school and walked out the front door to college, Larry and Beth's relationship did also.

As a psychologist in clinical practice for over twenty years, I have witnessed an explosion of divorces among those couples who had been married for twenty years or longer. They are called "empty-nest divorces." However, God did not design marriage to be this way. In Genesis 2:24, we can see that the system was designed for the kids to leave and the parents to stay: "Therefore a man shall leave his father and mother and be joined to his wife, and they shall become one flesh."

As the kids move out, the marriage moves on.

It's Time to Make a Case for Good Parents, Great Partners—How Did We Get This Way?

The year was 1918 and twenty million deaths worldwide were attributed to a deadly disease called influenza. In the United States alone, more than five hundred thousand people lost their lives to this acute respiratory disorder. Similar to this horrendous epidemic, a disorder in America is spreading like wildfire among the households of well-intentioned but misguided parents. Their children are being threatened by a devastating and debilitating condition that few psychologists are trained to diagnose, fewer physicians are prepared to treat, and no medical interventions have been developed to cure.

This syndrome is called "affluenza."

For some time now, kids have become the center of our attention, the center of our families, and the center of our culture. Parents from every social and economic class are doing *everything* they can for their kids in an effort to provide them with the pieces of the puzzle they missed when they were growing up. Parents offer them every opportunity for success and every occasion to improve themselves. As a result, their kids' dreams and desires are driving many parents into emotional, financial, and physical ruin. Take a look around...in many families, the kids have progressed from family members to family management!

The child-centered circus is popular these days—moms and dads compare their toddlers' trophies and their adolescents' achievements. This transition began in the sixties and seventies, when the baby boom was taking off and well-meaning parents turned their backs on Scripture and their attention toward Dr. Spock. He suggests that parents create a democracy in which everyone in the family is entitled to freedom of expression and freedom of choice. Parents were encouraged to sit cross-legged in their defiant toddler's playpen and reason with him. Historically we moved from parental dictatorship to parental default, and children became the center of the family. Unfortunately, few checked to see if this child-centric model was sanctioned by Scripture. I checked. It was nowhere to be found.

On a recent edition of the television program *20/20*, Connie Chung investigated the surprising effects of children growing up in well-to-do families in which the children had become the focus of the families. Psychotherapist Jessie O'Neill called this phenomenon "The Golden Ghetto." The Golden Ghetto results when family values are distorted and boundaries are blurred. She went on to say that many well-intentioned parents have created "child-focused" families, resulting in children who believe they're "entitled" to the good things in life and behave according to that belief. Most will grow up unable to tolerate frustration and unable to delay gratification. That's why we say:

PRINCIPLE #7:
Choose Marriage over Minors and "Couplehood" over Parenthood.

Spouse-Centered Families

Don't get me wrong. Neglect is not the answer. Yes, we love our kids, but love for kids was never designed to replace love for spouse. Healthy homes are centered upon a healthy husband/wife relationship, not upon the kids' social activities and personal ambitions. The heart of a marriage is centered on love and the hub of parenting is centered on leadership. Neither of these will succeed if your children's unrestricted schedules and unlimited desires drive parental decision-making.

The bottom line: If children are unclear about parent/child boundaries today, they are likely to demonstrate inappropriate employer/employee boundaries tomorrow. When children are robbed of healthy separation experiences today, they are likely to experience unhealthy separation anxiety tomorrow. Balance time spent with kids—and time spent with spouse.

Minimize marital drift by making marriage matter.

JENNI'S TIPS FROM THE TRENCHES… TO TURN THINGS AROUND

1. Celebrate Date Night weekly, not weakly.

Courtship can make a comeback when it's a priority rather than an afterthought. If money is an issue, remember that you don't have to fly first-class to an oceanfront condo at the Mauna Kea Beach Hotel in Hawaii to connect with your spouse. We have scheduled Friday nights as Date Night. A standing schedule can be made with a baby-sitter. Or to minimize cost, you can trade off sitting for some friends' kids every other weekend. Our fifteen-year-old daughter, Brittany, is now able to baby-sit for us on Friday nights, and she is then free to spend time with her friends on Saturdays and Sundays. Again, don't make money the issue; it's all about time—time to go for a walk, get an ice cream cone, go out for dinner, or see a movie.

2. Lock your bedroom door.

Step 1: Purchase—and install—a lock for your bedroom door. Step 2: Now use it! Sure, there are exceptions (e.g., when kids are ill), but it's hard to "get in the mood" when you're afraid a child might burst through the door at any moment wanting a glass of water. Bedrooms establish boundaries. Parents need time together. If an emergency occurs, the kids can knock on the door and explain their emergency. Thirst is not an emergency!

3. Put the kids to bed early.

The latest research from the National Institutes of Health suggests that most toddlers need at least ten to eleven hours of sleep each night, and adolescents need nine to nine and a half hours in order to meet the physical, emotional, and cognitive demands of their day.[1] Furthermore, I suggest that kids go to their bedrooms *before* bedtime (to read, play, slow down) for their benefit, as well as yours. Ask yourself, *How much time do my spouse and I need together at the end of each day?* Now do the math. This may mean that the kids head to their bedrooms at 10 P.M., 9 P.M., or even 8:30 P.M. It's a practice that will prove to be healthy for them…and wholesome for you.

4. Children have their own beds. Use them!

We don't believe in the concept of "group bed." There are exceptions, for example when small babies are in a bassinet or when kids are ill or scared because of a traumatic incident or nightmare. But generally speaking, children need to sleep in their own beds. Marriage is not a threesome, a foursome, or a group thing. Family is a group thing, which is why we eat together in the kitchen and play together in the family room, but bedtime is not a family thing. Teaching the importance of your relationship to your kids begins when you communicate to them that Mommy and Daddy have a special relationship and sleeping together is one of those things that makes it special. Chuck says that in family therapy it's called *enmeshment* when the boundary is not clearly defined. Separation is good; practice it.

5. Practice "parent time" daily.

There are two methods of "parent time" that can be incorporated into your family schedule every day, one before dinner and one after. The first occurs when Mom and Dad arrive home. After a brief time with each child, where kisses and hugs are offered in abundance, parents meet and talk about their day together. For us, this is usually a kitchen thing, and the kids are told, "Mommy and Daddy are going to spend the next fifteen to twenty minutes together to talk, so go play for a few minutes and don't come back in the kitchen—unless there's bloodshed."

Another "parent time" option is feasible if you have children over the ages of ten. Because Mom and Dad spent their time and resources purchasing and preparing supper, the kids are responsible to contribute to family life by cleaning up after the meal. Parents need to make good use of this time by going for a walk or sitting on the deck together, demonstrating that marriage really matters to Mom and Dad.

6. Limit extracurricular activities.

Kids' recreation options are limitless, and many parents fear that if they don't get their kids involved in every conceivable activity—with the best coach in town, at the earliest possible age—the window of opportunity will slam shut. Heaven forbid that the Olympic gold medal go to someone else or the recording contract with Capitol Records be lost forever! Here's the rule of thumb we suggest: one activity per child, per season—period. Try it. There may be exceptions—you may have a multitasking teen who can easily juggle school and a full plate of extracurricular activities—but keep in mind that we have seen too many worn-out parents with burned-out kids. In our household, we stick with the one-per-season rule.

7. Interruptions are by request, not by demand.

Not too long ago we interviewed Lisa Whelchel, best known for her role as "Blair" on the television show *The Facts of Life*. We talked with Lisa about her life as a sitcom star and now as a pastor's wife and mother of three. No longer on the set, she turned her attention to writing a book for parents called *Creative Correction*. In the book, Lisa shares how she solved her dilemma when her kids wanted her attention while she was on the phone, talking to a friend, or engaged in conversation with her husband, Steve. Her solution? The "Interrupt Rule." Lisa acknowledges that there are exceptions, but as a rule, her kids know: "If you want Mom's attention while she's busy, gently rest your hand on hers and she will acknowledge your request and lay her hand on top of yours. Then when there is a logical break in her conversation, Mom will give you a chance to speak."[2]

We think it's a great idea because it teaches consideration, boundaries, and priorities.

So how do parents raise healthy, wholesome kids these days?
The old-fashioned way—by building a fun, focused,
and fulfilling marriage!

Chapter Eight

WHEN CONVENIENCE IS VALUED...MORE THAN CREATION

Value Life—No Matter What the Cost.

*No matter how bad things get you got to go on living,
even if it kills you.*

SHOLOM ALEICHEM

*What will it profit parents if their kids gain a life of great value
yet fail to understand the great value of a life?*

LET'S TALK WITH JENNI

The words were out of my mouth before my mind was even in first gear. I sounded like a two-toothed farmer's wife telling the *National Enquirer* about an alien abduction.

"You know, I was just sitting there on the front porch, mindin' my own bizness, watchin' the corn grow, when I saw a flying saucer head straight for old Bessie, our prize-winnin' milkin' cow, don'tcha know. I shouted to Milton, 'Honey

Bun!' (That's what I call 'im when I really need 'im.) Get off that couch. We got comp'ny!' Well, by the time my Milton came out to the porch, those foreigners hit me with a beam of light brighter'n the lightbulb on the barn! And for the next nine months, I had this little alien creature livin' on my insides."

Well, you get the idea.

It was just before dinner one Saturday night. Chuck and I were entertaining our friends Greg and Emily, a young kid-less couple, when the subject of having a baby came up. They had been married for just over three years and had that twinkle in their eyes when they asked how having children had changed our lives. I was a few sentences into my "alien" story, when Chuck took Greg outside to check on the burgers.

On their way out I heard Chuck telling Greg that he had read a government study that calculated the cost for a middle-income family to raise a child from birth to eighteen to be $160,000. Talk about sticker shock! As Greg picked himself up off the floor, Chuck went on to say it wasn't that bad if you broke it down into payments—after all that's the American way. That translates to about $8,889 a year, $741 per month, or just $171 per week.

Greg was beginning to breathe again.

Chuck continued, saying that it cost a mere $24.35 a day, or just over a dollar an hour—per child! No wonder the researchers concluded that young couples were the last people on earth that could afford to consider parenthood!

I couldn't wait to get Emily's undivided attention. Her eyes were wide as saucers. I knew that money wasn't the issue for her as she dreamed about motherhood, so I put it in terms only a woman could understand. Being pregnant is just like having your body taken over by aliens, I told her. All of a sudden, there's a little "foreigner" inside your body causing all kinds of commotion. Basically, you have to accept that you've just lost control of your body from the chest down.

We're talking stretch marks, swollen feet, sore back, sleepless nights, and hourly trips to the bathroom! You'll gain weight you've never imagined possible and have every stranger in town pat your tummy and make cute remarks. Later on, this little creature will decide it needs more room and start to kick, shove, and stretch. And then it'll decide it likes the cozy little condo so much that it's going to extend its stay an extra two weeks!

About that time, the guys returned from the grill and pulled a couple of chairs up to the table. Greg looked at Emily…Emily looked at Greg…and I could tell that they were both overwhelmed with excitement and anticipation about having their own little bundle of joy!

That's when Chuck and I told them the rest of the story. We admitted that the numbers don't make sense and the stretch marks don't go away.

But all things considered, we wouldn't have it any other way!

While most of us have concluded that the pleasures of parenthood far outweigh the physical and financial price tag, some have decided to take a different pathway to family life.

Let's Talk with Chuck: A Baby Desired

Success is getting what you want.

Happiness is wanting what you get.

Michelle Bica had neither.

Thomas Bica, a corrections officer at the Portage County Jail, met Michelle in 1994 while she was serving time for possession of stolen property. Maybe that was a sign of things to come. After she was released, Thomas and Michelle were married, and shortly thereafter, Michelle suffered several miscarriages, which left her feeling barren and broken. She was emotionally troubled and maternally empty.

She felt like a surgeon without a scalpel, a person without a purpose, a woman with an empty womb.

Eventually, Michelle's despair turned to delight. The announcement was made in December 1999 that she would become a mother in September 2000. Michelle Bica was convinced that the new millennium was about to grant her a miracle.

From the beginning, Michelle openly shared her excitement and passion for parenthood, telling friends and family all about her medical updates and ultrasound results. She frequently had people feel her growing abdomen and showed her appreciation for each of the baby showers that were given in anticipation of the coming arrival.

With enthusiasm, Thomas and Michelle surveyed the birthing facilities at Akron General Medical Center. They met with a priest to arrange for their newborn to be christened and rented a hall for the much-anticipated celebration. The baby's room was ready and the expecting parents were filled with anticipation.

*But Michelle knew
that one crucial piece of the puzzle was missing.*

It fell into place when Michelle met Theresa Andrews in the infant department at a Wal-Mart in the sleepy suburb of Ravenna, just a few miles southeast of Cleveland, Ohio. Theresa was shopping for baby clothes. Michelle was shopping for a baby. Literally.

Michelle and Theresa talked casually about pregnancy, parenthood, and Pampers. They discovered that they lived just blocks from each other, and Theresa Andrews told Michelle Bica that she was expecting to give birth to a boy in about a month. Little did she know that this revelation would turn out to be her death sentence.

Michelle decided that a son would be just fine.

At five feet three inches tall and 180 pounds, Michelle's weight was her ally but the calendar was her enemy. She had deceived her husband, betrayed her friends, and abandoned her conscience.

*Her pregnancy was a sham.
Her "due date" was approaching.
And desperate times demanded desperate action.*

On September 27, 2000, Michelle lured Theresa to her home by pretending to purchase a Jeep from Theresa and her husband, Jon. Just inside the back door of her laundry room, Michelle used a handgun and fired a single shot to take Theresa's life. Moments later, she made an incision into

Theresa's abdomen—to take her baby.

Michelle performed a crude but effective cesarean section and delivered the newborn late that morning. She then buried Theresa's body under the dirt floor of the garage and cleaned up the bloody mess. By late afternoon Michelle called her husband to announce the good news. She told Thomas that she had been in too much pain to get to the hospital, so she had delivered her baby naturally in their home and he was now the proud father of a bouncing baby boy.

Oh yeah, mother and baby were doing fine.

Police Chief Randall McCoy determined that it took Michelle Bica less than five hours to accomplish this heartless crime and cover it up. In that short time, Michelle robbed a woman of her life, a husband of his wife, and a newborn baby of the chance to be cuddled in his mother's arms.[1]

This was a murder motivated by envy.

Our kids see headlines like this and wonder about the world they're growing up in. They assume these events are committed by unknown adults living in a faraway land. Surely this couldn't happen in their own backyard or be committed by someone their own age.

Then they hear the news that not far away another life has been stolen. This time over greed.

A Bicycle Demanded

A similar story takes place and another life is extinguished—this time in exchange for an eighty-nine-dollar bicycle.

Tina Blaylock, mother of four, had a "funny feeling" in her stomach that day. A feeling that something devastating was going to happen. She was right. "Something told me not to go to work today," she said. Unfortunately, it was already too late.

Tina worked as a dietary aide at a nursing home in Fort Worth, Texas. She was in the process of calling work to tell them she would not be in for her shift, but the exchange had already taken place. In the park less than a block down the street, her child lost his life—and a mother lost her son. While she was still on the phone, her younger children came running into the kitchen to tell her the ominous news.

Her next call was 911.

Moments earlier, her seventeen-year-old son, Marquis, had been leveled when a single bullet ripped through his chest. A two-day feud had taken its course. An impasse was reached. A gun was unveiled. A shot was fired. Marquis lay on the cold concrete sidewalk beside the jungle gym. Tina Blaylock ran to the aid of her dying son. She arrived just in time to plead with him to fight for his life, only to watch helplessly as he "took his last breath right before my eyes." As tears filled her eyes and horror filled her heart, she shrieked, "My son died over a bike!"

"What kind of sense does this make?" she asked. "None!" she replied to her own question as Marquis's lifeless body lay on her lap.

The assailants fled the scene but were quickly caught by the police. The suspects were neighbors. Two of the kids were sixteen years old. The third was only fourteen.[2]

Another life extinguished, not for envy, but for greed.

Kids killing kids? Unfortunately, this isn't just an isolated incident on a neighborhood playground, but another example of a child's life extinguished by a minor. Every day our kids are reminded of the horrors that happened in schools such as Columbine High School in Littleton, Colorado; Heath High School in Paducah, Kentucky; and Santana High School in Santee, California—schools that are better known for their slayings than for their scholars. The security measures in school yards today remind our kids daily that their classrooms are not exempt from violence. On Sunday, they hear that God is the Giver of life. On Monday morning, they have to wonder if they're sitting beside someone in their class who may be on the verge of stealing it.

No matter what the cause, our kids' perception of the value of life is diminished with each life lost. But as tragic as each incident is, the number of murders that were motivated by anger, envy, or greed pales in comparison to the number of lives that are taken for convenience.

Everywhere. Every day.

An Unborn Discarded

This holocaust occurs first in our hearts and then in our hospitals.

But this time we don't call the police.
It's not a crime.
We don't call the ambulance.
It's not an emergency.

We don't call the newspaper.
It's not a headline.
We call the doctor.
It's called pro-choice.

Although physicians call it a procedure, another life is extinguished; another life is terminated. Not out of anger or envy—this time it's for convenience.

Let's face it. Given the number of abortions performed in this land, the most dangerous place to live in America is not the ghetto. The most dangerous people among us are not drug-addicted criminals. And the most lethal weapon in America is not a gun. Unfortunately, the most dangerous place is a mother's womb. The most dangerous people are abortionists; the most dangerous weapons, doctors' instruments.

By the end of this year, another 1.1 million babies will be aborted, most within the walls of a doctor's office. Since 1973, 38–40 million babies have been aborted[3] by someone who took a pledge to save lives, not end them. And while most of us watch silently from the sidelines, conscience takes a backseat to convenience, and the condition of this nation's character falls another notch.

We wring our hands.
We curb our conscience.
We look the other way.

Unfortunately, the unborn have no union, no vote, and no lobbyists. Without a voice in Washington, they have little hope. If people were honest, they would see that their behavior lacks moral rationale:

If a child is left on a doorstep, it's called abandonment.
People are appalled.

If a baby is disposed of in a Dumpster, it's called murder.
People are horrified.

But if an unborn baby is aborted in its mother's womb, we call the Supreme Court.
They call it pro-choice.

On the sidelines, our kids sit and wonder about the value of a human life. It can be taken by a woman consumed by envy, a teen filled with greed, and a culture committed to convenience.

Envy. Greed. Convenience.

The symptoms are many.

The frequency is alarming.

The consequences can be everlasting.

That's why parents need to teach our kids to…

> ## PRINCIPLE #8:
> *Value Life—No Matter What the Cost.*

The value people place on life in the twenty-first century is in a freefall. But look carefully—envy, greed, and convenience have taken the lives of several before our time. This problem is not new:

- Driven by *envy,* Cain took Abel's life (Genesis 4:3–8).
- Driven by *greed,* Judas betrayed Jesus (Matthew 26:14–16, 48–49).

- Driven by *convenience,* David arranged for the death of Uriah (2 Samuel 11:4–5, 15).

It doesn't take a behavioral scientist to reveal that selfishness has always been at the center of our misguided behaviors. In today's culture it seems more prevalent, more popular, more pardoned.

Today we live in a culture that minimizes responsibility and maximizes personal rights. We have devalued life inside the womb and have depreciated life outside the womb. We openly ridicule authority and repeatedly mock those who sit in the highest office of the land. Disrespect and disregard are widespread. Students assault teachers in the classroom, and athletes blaspheme umpires on the diamond and referees on the court. Drivers disrespect police, road rage is commonplace, and air rage is on the rise.

Respect for others has taken a backseat while personal rights have moved to the front seat.

When the value of life is minimized, we rationalize taking a life when a baby is desired, killing a teen when a bike is demanded, aborting a baby when the situation is difficult.

As a couple, Jenni and I are convinced that people are precious and life is sacred, both in and out of the womb. Therefore, in our family we treat siblings with respect, we treat parents with regard, and we treat authority with reverence. As Christians, we're convinced that God is the giver of life: natural (Genesis 1:27), eternal (John 3:16), and abundant (John 10:10). Therefore, as followers of Christ we pray with our kids each night, thanking God for another day of life, asking Him for forgiveness that we might inherit eternal life, and seeking His blessing that we might experience abundant life.

As parents, we believe we can develop totally awesome kids by teaching them the value of life itself, rather than allowing them to settle for a life of "value." As a matter of fact, Cody asked us the other day just how much we thought he was worth to us. We said, "Cody, take it from us, we think you're worth a million dollars." Cody smiled and asked, "Well then, do you think you could advance me about twenty dollars of that for a new CD?"

Nice try!

JENNI'S TIPS FROM THE TRENCHES... TO TURN THINGS AROUND

1. Value life. It begins in the womb.

Teaching the value of life begins by valuing a baby in the womb. I talk openly to our children about the "baby growing in a woman's tummy." Notice that I use the word *baby*, not *fetus*. When our senior producer, Trish, was pregnant, it was a great opportunity for me to talk to my kids about how precious that baby was, how much her mommy loved her, and how fortunate her parents were to have a new baby coming into their family.

I remember having Dr. Neil Clark Warren, a well-recognized psychologist and author we have grown to love and admire, on our program. We asked him, "If you had unlimited resources and could give your child any one gift, what would it be?" He paused and said, "Forty-five months with the child's mother."

When I asked him what he meant by that, he said, "I'd give all children in America nine months inside their mother's womb—where Mom would take care of herself and prepare for her newborn, and the next thirty-six months outside the womb—where their mother could love, feed, and nurture them without the outside pressures of the world." To me, that's a wonderful example that teaches the value of life to our children better than any slogan, better than any speech, better than any sermon.

2. Value life by dealing with loss.

When a friend or family member dies, we think it's important to attend the funeral if at all possible. Obviously, age and emotional development are issues to consider. But generally speaking, if we minimize death by not attending the funeral, we give our children the message that this person's life was unimportant or insignificant. On the other hand, if we are overly distraught or emotionally devastated, we send the message that death is catastrophic and the grieving process is unbearable. This message implies that death is associated with horror and fear.

If possible, attend the funeral and use this occasion to talk about how much this person's life meant to you. Talk about how you're going to miss this person here on earth, but that you'll meet again because there is a place called heaven for people who have given their lives to God.

It's a great time to remind our kids that how one dies is not nearly as important as how one lives.

3. Value life by valuing boundaries.

Minimize an unplanned, unwelcome teenage pregnancy now. Go beyond the "birds and the bees" plumbing discussion and address teenage sexuality and sexual boundaries now. You may think it's too early, but better now than when it's too late!

When it comes to teaching our kids about sex, there seems to be a never-ending merry-go-round as parents look to the educational system, teachers look to the church, and the church looks to parents. The truth is that parents are primarily responsible for teaching their kids about sex, and the home is the best place for that to happen.

Home is the place to teach children that abstinence is still the best way to manage our sexuality before marriage—despite what they hear in the classroom or see on television. Sex education taught in the classroom teaches our kids how far they can go and how fast they can drive a car to the edge of a cliff—and still have time to stop. That's not good sex education, and it's not good driver's education either!

When Brittany began menstruating, it was a great opportunity not only to talk to her about all the dos and don'ts of starting her period, but also to underscore the reality that at age thirteen, she now had all the "parts in place" to become pregnant. She was flabbergasted! We talked about sexual purity and sexual boundaries and laid the foundation for an ongoing, open, and honest relationship that included discussing her sexual questions and challenges.

4. Value life by respecting others.

Chuck and I believe that *all* people deserve to be treated with respect, regardless of age or position. Parents teach respect to their children (and earn respect from their children) by modeling for them the act of treating all people (especially authority figures) with dignity and value. Teachers are greeted with a smile, police are met with honor, referees are given the final word—right or wrong.

That means we respect people's property, opinions, feelings, space, reputation, and body. We don't take things that aren't ours; we don't tell stories that aren't true; we don't hit people when we disagree. Instead we ask for help if there's a problem we can't solve. There is no shame in asking for help. We've always said, "Healthy kids ask for help." And healthy parents do too.

5. Value life by thinking before speaking and talking before acting.

Chuck and I are committed to teaching our kids to think before they speak and to talk before they act. We don't teach this just because Chuck's a psychologist, but because we know that we will save our kids much heartache if we teach them to process their thoughts before they express their words, and to know their feelings before they choose their behaviors.

Because words cannot be withdrawn after they've been spoken, Chuck and I constantly encourage our kids to think first and speak second—to mean what they say and say what they mean. Taking a few minutes to think things through before thoughts become words is seldom regretted. The rule is this: Bridle your tongue by filtering your thoughts.

Second, we need to provide a person, place, and time for our kids to talk about their feelings. The more they talk them out, the less they need to act them out. In most cases a parent will connect with the heart of their child, but some kids will connect better with a youth pastor, family member, friend, or counselor. Healthy parents recognize that *they* may not be the only people their kids feel comfortable with to work through their feelings. Rather than feeling threatened, thank God for sending someone special to stand in the gap for you. The most important issue here is not whom they share their feelings with but that their feelings are expressed rather than internalized (as most girls do) or thought through rather than acted upon (which is more typical for boys).

If you're looking for a "door opener" to get to your kids' feelings, you might want to say, "You know, if that happened to me I'd probably feel (angry, depressed, frustrated, lonely, etc.). Does that sound familiar?" Approaching them in this way gives your kids a chance to see you and themselves as similar and normal. Driving in the car is a great time to process issues with kids—they can't escape!

That's why God made cars!

6. Value life by living it abundantly!

John 10:10 is one of my favorite verses. It says, "I have come that they may have life, and that they may have it more abundantly." I wonder how many of us have accepted living in a gray world when God wants us to live in Technicolor.

I remember when Vestal Goodman told us about the deal she made with God when she gave her heart to Him. She said to the Lord, "I'll follow You for the rest of my life. I'll sing for You, I'll preach for You, I'll go wherever You want me to go…but in return I want Your full anointing. If I give You my all, I want Your all for me."

I've never forgotten that "deal" Vestal told us about, and

many times I've prayed the same prayer myself—*God, I want it all.*

What about you?

Don't hold back. Life was meant to be lived on the playing field, not on the sidelines. Your kids are counting on you to teach them how to "get in the game"—and how to play to win.

7. Value life by progressing from your past. Break the cycle.

There's no question about it—some families are caught in a vicious cycle of destruction. Generation after generation, family members continue to repeat the same mistakes and suffer the same consequences. It could be anything from alcoholism, divorce, drug addiction, depression, financial mismanagement, suicide, or any other self-defeating behavior. According to Chuck, the most frequent causes are biological, spiritual, or learned behavior.

Although there is considerable research suggesting the biological basis for disorders like depression, schizophrenia, and alcoholism, many of the behavioral patterns we demonstrate are learned from those who have gone before us.

If you can see a repeated pattern of self-destructive behavior in your own life, I encourage you to see a Christian mental health professional to help you find the cause of the behavior and determine a course of treatment. You've heard it before, "If you keep on doing what you've always done, you'll keep on getting what you've always got." If the cake always comes out of the oven flat, why use the same ingredients again tomorrow? Don't stay the course if you don't like the consequences.

Change the recipe or visit the bakery.

P.S. Oh, by the way, remember Greg and Emily, the childless couple described in the beginning of the chapter? Well, today they are the proud parents of a beautiful baby boy...and girl. Twins! I didn't realize that the twinkle in her eye meant that there were twins in her womb. Isn't that just like God?

Chapter Nine

WHEN LIFE IS LIVED BY CHANCE...RATHER THAN BY CHOICE

Choose Design over Default,

and Experience the Power of Purpose.

Begin with the end in mind.

STEPHEN R. COVEY

If you don't know where you are going,
you'll probably end up somewhere else.

LAURENCE J. PETER

LET'S TALK WITH JENNI

Living thousands of miles from my sister and mom, I always felt that it was hard for us to connect. That changed several years ago when we moved to Toronto. Despite the "border thing," we were only 219 miles (not that I was counting) from my sister in Ohio. I was elated! Shortly after we moved, I got a call from her. Her reason for calling was too good to be true!

"Please," she said, "let me take your kids for a week."

Now I know that most of you would jump at the chance to have a week alone without your kids, but I wasn't so eager. My kids had never been away from home for more than a night or two, and I worried about them getting homesick—or I should say worried about me getting "kid-sick."

My sister persisted and I finally gave in. I talked to the kids about their upcoming adventure, but I could tell they were feeling anxious too. To prepare my sister, I called and told her our concerns, and the next day we received the following fax:

Welcome to Camp Julie!

We are delighted that you have chosen to entrust your children to our care. In order to provide the best quality environment for your young campers, I ask that you review the following list of rules with your children.

1. Bubblegum will be given out at random and must be blown, twirled, stretched, and played with throughout the entire time it is in your child's mouth. Should the gum become accidentally embedded in their clothing, the carpeting, or the dog, bonus points will be given.

2. There will be no breakfast until each child has consumed at least one candy bar of his or her choice.

3. All green vegetables are strictly prohibited.

4. A minimum of five minutes per day must be spent jumping on the bed of his or her choice.

Well, the list went on, but I think you get the idea. It was obvious that Julie intended to spoil the kids rotten. During the next few weeks we received several more faxes detailing an array of activities and field trips for our kids to select from. Then, just before "Camp Julie" was to begin, we received a detailed daily schedule (in triplicate!) that ran from 8 A.M. to 8 P.M., listing every daily event. Julie even listed "Missing Mommy Time" projects for when our kids felt lonely or homesick. It was unbelievable!

Now, I don't want you to get the idea that my sister is an irresponsible party animal. She gave 100 percent to the kids and expected certain things in return. She adhered to a strict bedtime, required simple chores (like making their bed and cleaning up their toys), and expected one hour of quiet time each day.

To my surprise, their apprehension was replaced with exhilaration, and they were soon having the time of their lives. What made the difference? My sister minimized their fear of the unknown. She had a plan. Before they even left home, they knew where they were going, what they would do, and what was expected of them.

It was the plan that provided great peace.

As I watched what took place, I discovered that my sister knew the key to a successful week with my kids—and a principle of successful parenting for moms and dads. I was reminded that we make many of our parental choices without a purpose, direction, or destination in mind. As a weary parent, I have often made choices designed for tension-relieving rather than goal-achieving. While our kids were with Julie, I realized the importance of focus, goal-setting, and planning. These important factors gave my kids great peace, great purpose, and great pleasure.

By the way, in case you're wondering, after my sister had *spoiled* my kids to death, I needed almost a week to get them back to a regular schedule! Little does my sister know…two can play this game. I plan on picking up a drum set for her son's next birthday.

LET'S TALK WITH CHUCK: THE POWER OF PURPOSE

The truth is that most people today aren't who they want to be, living where they want to live, or raising their kids the way they think they should.

So now what?

Many of us live lives of quiet resignation because our personal, professional, and parental lives have fallen short of the expectations we envisioned earlier in life.

Despite the resources that are available to Christians today—from modest bookstores to media broadcasts, from seminars to psychologists—many marital relationships remain shallow, careers are at a standstill, and family relationships are stagnant. Still, few people will pull their vehicles to the side of the road and ask *why.* At the end of the day, many will discover that they have been dropped off at an undesirable destination or have run out of gas at an unwanted location. Most are left with diminished dreams and increased despair.

Our goals are unmet. Our priorities are unclear.
Our focus is undefined.

In many cases, we don't know where we're going, so it doesn't matter where we are or how we got here. Without a clearly defined destination, goal-achieving takes a backseat to tension-relieving. Just ask Tom Harken....

Driven by a Deficit

Most would have thought that Tom Harken was on the right road. He was accomplished professionally, recognized socially, and secure financially. While he was persistent in his behavior and prosperous in his business, he pressed forward because he felt ashamed when he looked back. He eventually overcame adversity and achieved great success, but he was a man driven by a deficit rather than by a dream.

On a warm spring day in 2000, we met Tom on the set of *At Home—Live*. Instantly, we were impressed by the contagious sparkle in his eye and the gentle embrace of his spirit. But he wasn't always like that.

Tom had been afflicted with polio at age eight, and after a lengthy hospitalization, he was then diagnosed with tuberculosis. He need more treatment, which meant he was unable to attend school for years. When he finally returned to school, he was "a very big kid in a very small desk." Unable to read or write and too far behind to catch up, at school Tom was like a square peg in a round hole. He was ripe for ridicule from his classmates, and his teachers failed to come to his defense. Filled with frustration and shame, Tom quit school at age thirteen, accepting the fact that he would have to face the world as a young man who could not read or write.

His disability remained a secret. It would drive him to succeed miraculously at work—but fail miserably at home.

As a dropout, Tom was driven to prove himself at work. Employed by his father in the family grocery store, Tom worked long and hard. He was unrelenting: determined to outwork, outsmart, and outrun his deficiency. He avoided the phone because he was unable to write down a customer's order, but his enthusiastic personality charmed most customers when face-to-face. Looking for approval and longing for acceptance, Tom honed his skills in the aisles of the grocery store. However, his secret forced him to cut corners. His father didn't know the cause, but he saw the consequences of his son's illiteracy. Within a year, the collapse of their relationship led to Tom's departure. He left for Florida—at age fourteen.

Unfortunately, his fortune was not to be found in Florida, so Tom returned home within a year. The fracture between father and son grew worse. At age fifteen, Tom met a seventeen-year-old girl and married her shortly thereafter. Now with a wife at his side, Tom sought a position with the Air Force. Because he failed every test required for entrance, he was classified as "uneducable and untrainable." To his surprise, though, he was classified as fit for the United States Air Police—*in the munitions department.*

Two children later and divorce papers now in hand, Tom met and married "Miss Melba." It was still apparent that his life was one of accident rather than arrangement. Although functionally illiterate, Tom kept his secret hidden and found success in the world of sales. As he secured orders, Tom would memorize the purchase and ask others to fill out the paperwork. Door-to-door vacuum sales were his specialty, but a wall-to-wall vacuum filled his life. His second marriage was no better than the first.

To this point, his life was more about problem-avoiding than goal-achieving.

Then, what should have been an occasion to remember turned out to be a night to forget. Melba was taken to the hospital in labor, ready to deliver their firstborn son. When they arrived at the hospital, nurses rushed Melba to the delivery room and directed Tom to the admitting desk. There he was asked to fill out Melba's admission forms.

He was face-to-face with his worst fear.

Would this be the day he was found out? Gripped by terror and reexperiencing the trauma and ridicule he felt when he returned to school at age thirteen, Tom's palms began to sweat. He understood little on the forms that stared at him.

He could fill in his name. Not much more. He was horrified. He froze. He stood helpless.

Fearful of being discovered, he ran. He ran just like many of us the day we were caught with our hand in the cookie jar…

- the day we were criticized by our supervisor and felt unqualified? We ran.
- the day we were challenged by our spouse and felt unwanted? We ran.
- the day we were confronted by the Holy Spirit and felt unworthy? We ran.

Tom rushed past the nurses' station, out of the waiting

room, and to his car. He ran back to the only world where he felt comfortable—his office. When the door was locked and the lights were off, tears rolled down his cheeks. Tears for Melba, tears for his newborn son, tears for himself. He was AWOL and his wife and son were in the hospital, alone.

Tom's departure left his family deserted and him disheartened— but his disability continued to drive his decision-making.

Apologies were made, but his absence continued. Escaping to work and to the pool hall, Tom avoided his needy family until one night his financial mismanagement meant that his newborn son was drinking sugar water instead of formula. With head bowed in shame, Tom whispered three words that changed his life. These three words became the start of a life driven by focus rather than by fear.

"I need help."

From vacuum sales to auto agency to restaurant owner, Tom became more and more successful in the workplace. He was focused, goal-directed, and intentional. He made deals during the day and learned how to read and write at night. Melba tutored Tom, beginning with *See Spot Run* and progressing to *Speech Writing 101*. That's right, Tom had learned to write a speech, and the first speech he wrote was one that he was to deliver *in Washington!*

Because of his business success, on May 1, 1992, Tom Harken was invited to the Grand Hyatt in Washington, D.C., to receive the Horatio Alger Award. In attendance were dignitaries like Dr. Henry Kissinger, Justice Clarence Thomas, and

General Colin Powell. Prior to the gala, Tom gathered his children together and shared with them that while they were growing up, he was falling down. He told them that he had been illiterate, unable to read or write. He explained that he had avoided them during the evenings because he was unable to help them with the simplest of homework assignments. He described to them how his driving force had been his disability. They were flabbergasted, but now some of the missing pieces made sense to them. This time with his family turned out to be a dress rehearsal for his announcement in Washington.

Tom Harken was given the Horatio Alger Award because of his public achievements—but that day he shared with his audience what had once been his private secret. Those in attendance sat spellbound. He told them of the pain and the price tag he had paid to keep his illiteracy hidden. His secret now known to his family and friends, Tom went on to publish a book entitled *The Millionaire's Secret* that told of his shame, his secret, and his newfound purpose in life: to stamp out illiteracy.[1]

Dr. Kissinger later told Tom that out of the thousands of speeches he had heard throughout his lifetime—most made by presidents and kings—only five were memorable to him. Tom's was one of them.

At age fifty-five, Tom Harken was no longer careless, reckless, or aimless. Tom Harken shared his secret and is no longer driven by his desire to cover up his deficit. Today, Tom is driven by the purpose in front of him, rather than by the problem behind him.

It's never too late to parent with purpose. That's why we believe in…

> ## PRINCIPLE #9:
> ### *Choose Design over Default, and*
> ### *Experience the Power of Purpose.*

Live by Choice, Not by Chance.

In its advertising campaign a few years ago, Microsoft asked the unthinkable question: "Where do you want to go today?" The implication was that if you could dream it, Microsoft could help you achieve it. Unfortunately, most of us are stuck at the fork in the middle of the road, defined by our problems rather than driven by our purpose.

> *Yogi Berra once said,*
> *"When you come to a fork in the road, take it."*

Alice was someone who could have used such advice. She lived in Wonderland and obviously never met Mr. Berra. When she arrived at the famous junction, she asked the Cheshire Cat for advice. "Cheshire Puss, would you tell me, please, which way I ought to go from here?"

"That depends a good deal on where you want to get to," said the Cat.

"I don't much care where—" said Alice.

"Then it doesn't matter which way you go," said the Cat.[2]

It's too late to think about where you want to go after you've arrived somewhere else. It's too late to think about what you want to buy once the money has been spent. It's too late to think about what you want to do with your life once your days are numbered. That was the case of an insightful eighty-five-year-old woman who had little time left to live, but insights left to share. She put it this way:

If I Had My Life to Live All Over Again

If I had my life to live all over again, I would make more mistakes in this life, not less. I would relax more. I would limber up. I would be sillier during this trip called life.

If I had my life to live all over again, there would be fewer things I would take so seriously. I would take more chances. I would take more trips. I would climb more mountains and swim more rivers. I would eat more ice cream and eat less beans.

If I had my life to live all over again, I'd have more actual troubles and fewer imagined ones. I would travel lighter on this trip called life. I'd stop living so far ahead of my time. I'd go barefoot earlier in the spring and stay that way later in the fall.

If I had my life to live all over again, I'd ride more merry-go-rounds. I'd watch more sunsets. I'd play more often with children. I'd go to more dances. I'd pick more daisies.

There would be a lot of things I'd do differently if I could live my life all over again, but you see, I can't.

NADINE STAIR[3]

These words hit close to home for many of us. We may be praiseworthy but not purposeful if we live by chance and not by choice. Living life without purpose is living life by the "ready, fire, aim!" philosophy.

For whatever a man sows, that he will also reap.

(GALATIANS 6:7)

On the other hand, imagine that you are eighty-five years old and have lived a life of purpose and productivity. Now let me ask you:

1. What made it so?
2. What are you doing *today* to make that dream happen?

The truth is that most of us would rather play than plan. Oh sure, some of us will whisper a prayer here and there asking God to direct our paths. But few of us will sit down and ask God to help us determine our purpose or define our plan. As a result, we miss out on a future designed by the Divine.

Who needs a plan?

Everyone who knows it's best to measure twice, cut once. Everyone who realizes it's best to draft a blueprint before building a house. Everyone who pens a thought before beginning a speech. Everyone who is honest and answers yes to any of the following:

1. Do you feel personally, professionally, or parentally aimless?
2. Do you feel like your world manages you, rather than you managing it?
3. Do you find yourself exhausted at the end of the day, with little to show for your efforts?
4. Do you find yourself procrastinating because you don't know where to start?

5. Do you feel guilty about the "shoulds" that seldom get accomplished?
6. Do you feel as though life is passing you by while others are progressing ahead?

If you answered yes to any of these, I have a question for you:

> *If you don't have the time to do something right,*
> *when do you think you'll find time to do it over?*

Todd Duncan, author of *The Power to Be Your Best*,[4] has been a guest on the program several times and has shared with us that in order to arrive at the right destination, at the right time, with the right people, there are three critical elements: person, purpose, and plan. If we examine these in more detail, they look like this...

CORE FEATURE	CRITICAL TRAIT	CENTRAL FACTOR
The right person	Character	Principle-centered
The right purpose	Passion	Mission-driven
The right plan	Purpose	Intentional

Therefore, if we hope to live up to our potential and return to God the highest interest on His investment in our lives, we must be people of character who are passionate about our calling and focused on the purpose (or destination) that God has called us to.

The apostle Paul put it this way:

But one thing I do, forgetting those things which are behind and reaching forward to those things which are ahead, I [reborn as a person of character] press [passionately] toward the goal [purpose] for the prize of the upward call of God in Christ Jesus. (Philippians 3:13–14)

Parental Purpose and Passion

During one of those difficult days, all parents will ask themselves, "What's the point of parenting anyhow?" Good question.

David Seel Jr., another guest who has visited with us on the set of *At Home—Live,* is author of the book *Parenting without Perfection.* In it, he offers ten purposes of parenthood. They include:

1. To model Jesus.
2. To pray for our children daily.
3. To demonstrate a life of integrity.
4. To set safe and appropriate boundaries.
5. To be a student of our children's world.
6. To promote our child's unique interests.
7. To encourage a passionate desire for Truth.
8. To respect their abilities and self-determination.
9. To influence their beliefs, rather than control their behaviors.
10. To shape their environment, because it will influence their heart.[5]

Now they tell us!

The power of purpose will make the difference between

those who want to make a living and those who want to make a difference. Let me encourage you to live life to the fullest and return to the Lord the highest interest on His investment in your life. In order to do so, you must live a life that is character-centered, passionate about your calling, and intentional in your planning. Secondly, you must teach your kids to live life in the same manner.

> *The secret to making things happen in life is to live intentionally and on purpose.*
> OREL HERSHISER, MVP AND WORLD SERIES CHAMPION

JENNI'S TIPS FROM THE TRENCHES... TO TURN THINGS AROUND

1. Become principle-centered and mission-minded.

Dr. Paul Faulkner, author of *Raising Faithful Kids,* cites a study that focused on six major corporations who attempted to identify common factors that lead to success.[6] The study revealed two factors that accounted for an eight-fold increase in the success rate when compared to their peers. They were clearly defined core principles and a focused mission.

By becoming principle-centered and mission-minded, you will increase your likelihood of success in the boardroom *and* the family room. The bottom line? Increase your success by parenting with intention, purpose, and direction.

> *I'd rather ride in a VW that knows where it's going than in a Lexus that's wandering around.*
> WILLIAM BENNETT

2. Resist the "someday syndrome."

Let's be honest, you probably said something like this again last week:

- "Once the kids begin school, I'm going to get serious about exercising."
- "When our children are older, we'll be able spend some time together."
- "As soon as the mortgage is paid off, we'll be able to go back to school."
- "Once I retire, we'll be able to take that trip we've always dreamed about."

Sound familiar? Admit it. You're suffering from the "someday syndrome."

Well, for those who have been stricken with this modern-day malady, here's a quick and easy suggestion from the best-selling authors Jack Canfield, Mark Victor Hansen, and Les Hewitt. It's taken from their latest book, *The Power of Focus.*[7] They suggest that for the outcome to change, we have to change—or else nothing much will change. They suggest the "Ta-Da" formula for those who feel stuck:

T Think about the options.
A Ask others for information.
D Decide today with the information you have.
A Act tomorrow by taking one step in the right direction.

And as W. L. Bateman said, "If you keep on doing what you've always done, you'll keep on getting what you've always got."

3.   Choose goal-achieving over tension-relieving.

As you know, there are times when life's troubles can be fixed by a warm bubble bath—and a family that is temporarily in another zip code visiting your in-laws! But because these times are few and far between, parents often find themselves making impulsive decisions that are based on what would be easier, rather than on what is best. I know. I've been there.

The problem with this is that most short-term, tension-relieving solutions often become long-term, stress-producing problems. There are times when we opt for immediate gratification (like buying things we can't afford as long as the payments are spread over the next four decades), but principle-centered parents *must* resist the tendency to be financially, emotionally, spiritually, and parentally short-sighted.

Instead, define your goals, share your goals, and maintain your goals regardless of the effort and in spite of the costs.

Convenience today that results in tension tomorrow is the way of the world...not the way of the wise.

4.   It's about focus, not hocus-pocus.

Most of us would like to cross our fingers and wish ourselves into a better life, but the answer is not hocus-pocus but focus. Rather than being driven by a problem, choose to be driven by a purpose. Set clearly defined individual and family goals. While there are many resources in the marketplace designed to help set goals, here are a few points that are common to most:

1. Your most important goals must be *yours.*
   This sounds obvious, but one of the most common mistakes made is to develop our goals based on what others want for us. Are they your goals or theirs?

2. Goals must be godly.
   Why settle for less?

3. Goals must be specific and measurable.
   A goal without a specific target or destination is not a goal; it's a slogan. Be specific, be exact, and establish time deadlines.

4. Goals must be out of immediate reach, but not out of sight.
   Goals that are too easy to achieve are effortless. Goals that are unattainable are exhausting: Neither will bring out your best in you or your family.

5. Goals must be balanced.
   Set goals that are realistic and focused on the things that matter most. For us that's faith, family, and friendships.

And remember, the first two letters of the word goal spell GO!

5. Learn the power of purpose.

A young, optimistic boy named Robert believed that if you could dream it, you could do it. He grew up on a dead-end dirt road with no name, in a house with no number, and in a bedroom with no electricity. At age five, Robert had a dream to become a preacher. He practiced his trade on the only congregation available—a herd of cows eating their way across a farm field. His first real congregation in 1955 was a group of a hundred that met in their cars at a drive-in movie theater. He knew them by the make of their cars, not by the contours of their faces or color of their hair.

Twenty years later, he shared with his congregation (which now numbered seven thousand) his dream to build the first all-glass church, in Garden Grove, California. On September 14, 1980, Pastor Robert Schuller stepped behind the pulpit of the Crystal Cathedral—and gave evidence to his "possibility" theology.

On the wall in his office hangs a plaque with an acrostic that symbolizes his "power of purpose" philosophy. It is based on the word *strive:*

S   Start Small
T   Think Big
R   Reach Beyond Yourself
I   Invest Everything You Have
V   Visualize Your Miracle
E   Expect Success

As a counselor to presidents, a pastor to thousands, and an inspiring voice to millions of television viewers, Robert Schuller proved that with a clearly defined purpose and a passion to see it fulfilled, God can take you from nowhere to anywhere.

6.   Parent with purpose.

There's no question about it, the number one reason most people fail to achieve their goals is because they never set them in the first place!

Most people will spend more time planning a Christmas party than they will spend time planning their life!
DENIS WAITLEY

Set goals: short-term, yearly, and lifetime. Get focused, measure your progress, and witness God's provision in your life. If the method for doing this leaves you floundering, try filling in this chart. It identifies ten of the most important areas of life in which people need goals:

AREA	ONE-MONTH GOAL	ONE-YEAR GOAL	LIFETIME GOAL
PERSONAL			
MARITAL			
PARENTAL			
FAMILY			
SPIRITUAL			
PROFESSIONAL			
FINANCIAL			
PHYSICAL			
RECREATIONAL			
SOCIAL			

Long-range goals are important—they keep us from becoming frustrated by short-term failures. Chuck and I believe that if you will take a chance and "fill it in," God will have a chance to "fulfill it in." If you see goal-setting as simply another opportunity for failure, let me ask you who the failure is: someone who accomplishes 50 percent of something or someone who accomplishes 100 percent of nothing?

Eighty-five-year-old Nadine Stair lived by chance rather than by choice.

What about you?

For most of his life, Tom Harken was driven by a problem rather than by a purpose.

What about you?

Your children have a chance to discover the power of purpose.

They need their parents to show them how.

Chapter Ten

WHEN THEIR HEREAFTER IS IN YOUR HANDS...

Why Give Them the World When You Can Offer Them the Word?

For what will it profit a parent to gain the whole world and lose their child for eternity?

LET'S TALK WITH JENNI

It was Saturday morning, 8:01 A.M. Our bedroom door squeaked open, and there they stood at the edge of the bed. Their presentation was flawless. Performing with the precision of an Olympic relay team, they passed the verbal baton back and forth like seasoned gold medalists.

To Brittany it was an issue of humanity: "We need to set them free." To Cody it was the well-being of our home: "We need one to make us a family." To Courtney it was an issue of the heart (hers): "I would really be happy if we got one."

Charts were drawn. Graphs were presented. Tasks were allocated.

These kids were pros.

Even that early in the morning, Chuck and I realized that the kids had us in the palms of their hands. The outcome was inevitable. The time had come.

And so it was that our content little family of five was about to increase by one. The light was green; the search was on. We were now on the hunt for the "perfect puppy."

Now there's an oxymoron!

I knew it wasn't going to be easy. I love my husband dearly, but when it comes to purchases over fifty dollars, he can be, well, obsessive. Early one spring we needed a basic garden hose for the backyard. A simple task, I thought—a quick trip to Home Depot, grab a hose, and go, right?

Wrong!

Chuck surveyed Wal-Mart, Kmart, Home Hardware, Ace Hardware, Lowe's, True Value, Home Depot, and Bud's Farm Supply. Comparisons were made. Warranties were examined. Finally he was ready to make a purchase, to risk it all, to take the plunge—to part with part of his paycheck. By then it was October!

I used to admire his cautious consumerism.
Now it's just plain irritating.

We traveled to pet stores. We visited breeders. We scanned the Internet. Of course, I fell in love with everything that had fur, four legs, and a tail. Chuck was not quite so easily charmed.

At the twentieth pet store we had visited within a 250-mile radius, Courtney suddenly announced, "I want this one." We looked at her. Snuggled in the arms of our six-year-old daughter was a puppy that looked like two pounds of wrinkles. There was fur, but no frame—it looked like someone had let the air out of this canine and all that was left was a fur coat.

The experts called her a Chinese shar-pei.
Courtney called her "Playdough."
Chuck took one look at the price tag and called our banker.

While Chuck was securing a loan, I was starting a list. I had a mission in mind. I had to transform a person-centered home into a pet paradise. Nothing was too good for this new bundle of joy. She was family. Her comfort was our priority. Cost was no object. PetSmart was the place.

First, a bed—nothing but the best would do. A heated, orthopedic pet bed by Snuggle Safe with a custom-fit, 100 percent sheepskin pet pad and a color-coordinating velveteen pillow would be great. For dinner, it would be PetSmart Premier high-protein, oven-baked chicken meal with Omega-3 and Omega-6 fatty acids served in a designer PetZazz elevated food bowl. For dessert, a round of Milk-Bone's soft and chewy bacon and cheese treats, followed by a few Gingerbread Bark Bars, Purina Right Bites, and Alpo Chicken Strips.

For evening fun, we needed a Rhino Super-Tug chew toy, which would gently massage and clean her gums as we pulled and played. And for that after-supper evening stroll, we needed a Companion Road, 100 percent cotton, machine-washable Fido sweater to fend off the chill in the air; a Top Paw black-leather and diamond collar; and a Spot Light retractable leash that offered the latest in canine comfort and control. The bill: $378.45!

Chuck's going to pass out when he sees this bill!

As time passed, we soon discovered that Playdough would rather eat the scraps from our table than the high-protein food in her bowl. She'd rather chew on the shoes in our closet than play with the trinkets in her toy box. She'd rather be warmed by the coat on her back than by a dog-sweater from the store.

Over the years, Playdough has taught us a lot about parenting a puppy.

- She wants more of our time and less of our toys.
- She longs for more of our love and less of our luxuries.
- She hungers for more of our attention and less of our assets.

Something tells me that most kids want the same.

Let's Talk with Chuck: More Than We Need, but Not What We Want

We offered Playdough the pleasures of pet paradise, yet something was still missing. We provided Playdough with the equivalent of a Beverly Hills mansion—furnished. Cooks in the kitchen, maids in the den, and a Ferrari in the garage. That should have done it, but it didn't. She had more than she needed, but not what she wanted.

She wanted less comfort and more closeness.

I remember counseling a mother of four. She was forty-seven years old and disillusioned. Again. In her marriage, she was about to exchange the words *I love you* for *I'm leaving you.* To most people, she had more than enough—enough to fill a five-bedroom home on a hillside, enough for the Lexus in the driveway and private schools for her kids. *But it wasn't enough.* Her marriage was loveless. Her church left her lifeless. Her life felt pointless. She wanted to be loved. She wanted to be needed. She wanted her life to be meaningful. On the outside, she had more than she needed. On the inside, it wasn't what she wanted.

She wanted less luxury and more love.

Then there's the story in the Gospel of Luke about the young man who had all that he needed but not what he *wanted* (15:11–32). Jesus tells this story about the son of a wealthy man who traded in his future for a pound of pleasure. He insisted on his fair share of the family fortune and traveled to a faraway place, seeking to trade in his *dull life* for the *dazzling life.* He dropped his denarii on the table and purchased a pound of prodigal living. But the dazzle didn't last. When his money ran out, so did his friends and so did his options.

His riches were squandered.
His stomach was empty.
His shoulders were weary.

They were burdened by the burlap sack that carried his regrets. Now starving—and willing to trade pride for provisions—he returned home and fell into the arms of the one who offered him everything he needed: a fatted calf to fill his empty stomach, a spotless robe to cover his soiled past, a father's ring to restore his family heritage.

Isn't that just like God? He knows our wants—but delivers our needs. He's willing to offer us everything we need in exchange for what little we have. He offers us the opportunity to dine on the Bread of Life when all the world has to offer is a slice of life.

For each of these examples, a principle can be applied—a principle that considers not only the earthly but also the eternal. A principle that can be applied in the lives of those:

- who have offered their kids all the comforts of the world,
- who have offered their spouse all the luxuries of the world,
- who have witnessed a wayward loved one experience all the short-term pleasures of the world.

Parents need to consider:

> ## PRINCIPLE #10:
> *Why Give Them the World*
> *When You Can Offer Them the Word?*

God understands the longings of a puppy (and of a people) who lives in the Land of Plenty and has "everything," but misses the warmth of its master's heart. In fact, God hungers for an intimate relationship with those who'd prefer more closeness and less comfort. The Word says:

I love those who love me,
And those who seek me diligently will find me.
(Proverbs 8:17)

God understands the longings of a woman living in the Land of Prosperity, who aches for the love of her spouse. God wants to care for and comfort those who'd prefer more love and less luxury. The Word says:

I will make you my wife forever, showing you righteousness and justice, unfailing love and compassion. (Hosea 2:19, NLT)

God understands the sorrow of a misguided prodigal, fresh from the Land of Pleasure, who longs for the family he left and the heritage he squandered. God desires to restore what was lost and rebuild what was wasted. The Word says:

And I will restore to you the years that the locust hath eaten. (Joel 2:25, KJV)

If you desire to propel your kids beyond the ways of the world:
Offer them the Word...
- for every headache (Proverbs 3:5–6)
- and every heartache (Isaiah 58:9).

Offer them the Word...
- for every fear (2 Timothy 1:7)
- and every failure (2 Chronicles 30:9).

Offer them the Word...
- for every weakness (1 Corinthians 10:13)
- and every worry (Matthew 6:34).

If you want more for your family than what the world has to offer, *give them the Word.* You'll give them hope on earth and a home in heaven. But the longer you wait, the more difficult the work.

According to researcher George Barna, if young people do not accept Jesus Christ as Savior before the age of eighteen, the likelihood of them ever doing so is slim. How slim? Once our kids turn nineteen, there's only a 6 percent chance that they will ever make a decision to follow Jesus.[1] That's slim!

Still wondering about the impact of the world and the importance of the Word?

Desiring the World but Delivering the Word

Let's be honest, most of us are looking for *more.*

Kids want...	more playtime in their daytime
	more clothes in their closet
	more money for the mall
	more activities for their weekend.
Parents want...	more credit for their card
	more romance for their marriage
	more patience for their parenting
	more time for their family.

The world suggests that personal fulfillment and parental success are found in "more." The Word tells us that true fulfillment and success are found only in God. The world suggests that life is an outside-in process: Get more, need less. The Word tells us that life is an inside-out process: Get God, need nothing. Unfortunately, many parents and teens have been searching on the outside for something that's missing on the inside. We've been searching under the streetlight rather than looking in the "Sonlight."

There's a story about a man who was on his hands and knees, searching for something under the streetlight, when a friend came by and asked, "Hey, what are you looking for?"

"Oh," the man said, "I'm looking for my house keys."

"Why don't you show me where you lost them and I'll help you find them?"

"I lost them on the driveway, somewhere between the garage and the front door," the man replied.

Confused, the friend asked, "Then why are you looking for your keys out here under the streetlight?"

"Well, that's easy. This is where the light is."

Now let me meddle for a moment.

What are you looking for? What are your kids looking for? And more important, are you looking under the streetlight or in the "Sonlight"?

Our kids are looking for direction. Our kids are hungry for truth. Our kids are longing for something more than fast-food answers to quench their innermost spiritual appetite. Instead, they're looking for a God who is reliable, relevant, and relational. They're looking for a faith that is firm in a world that is fragile. They're longing for a faith that can be counted on in a world that can't be. A faith that still fits when:

- friends leave,
- parents divorce,
- depression strikes,
- grandparents die,
- accidents happen.

*A faith like this can be found only in the Sonlight,
not under the streetlight. In the Word, not in the world.*

Quite frankly, many of us have looked to experts on *Oprah* and medicine men on infomercials. They're not enough. Never have been. Never will be. Not enough to satisfy the relationships we thirst for, the time we hunger for, the freedom we wish for, the significance we hope for, the goals we aspire to, the kids we pray for, or the families we long for.

We have looked in the Land of Plenty, the Land of Prosperity, and the Land of Pleasure. We've looked where it's convenient, rather than where it's critical. We've looked in the world rather than the Word. Sadly, our kids have followed our lead. But it's never too late for principle-centered parents to turn back the clock and take back their kids.

A LESSON LEARNED FROM A POOCH WITH PRIORITIES

When in doubt, I glance at the one who has it all. Playdough has more food than she hungers for, more water than she thirsts for, and more toys than she has time for. She has a bed she doesn't want. A collar she doesn't wear. A leash she doesn't like and a sweater she doesn't need.

She traded it all in for a place to rest at the foot of our bed, a place to eat at the foot of our table, and a place to walk at the foot of her master.

When all is said and done, our kids desire the same.

For the sake of their hearts and the sight of their hereafter, let me ask you again: Why give them the world when we can offer them the Word?

JENNI'S TIPS FROM THE TRENCHES... TO TURN THINGS AROUND

1. Deliver the goods.

   We've all been there...
   We've offered our kids:

   - fun, when their souls hungered for faith,
   - luxury, when their hearts longed for love,
   - toys, when their consciences searched for truth,
   - trinkets, when their hearts appealed for our time,
   - latitude, when they secretly craved limits,
   - information, when their minds were thirsty for wisdom.

   Therefore we want to encourage you to be parents who provide for your kids *fewer* of their wants but *all* of their needs. To look to the lasting and deliver the eternal. To provide the substance of Scripture and package it in faith, love, truth, time, limits, and wisdom.

2. Refuse to be driven by the world.

   You'll hear it at breakfast. You'll hear it at bedtime. And as if that's not enough, you'll hear it several times in between. You guessed it: "Everybody else has one! Why can't I?"

With this in mind, there are three critical points to communicate to your child. Repeat after me:

1. "I understand that there are some kids in your school who have one."

2. "I also know that there are some kids at your school who don't."

3. "You'll be a member of the second group!"

> *And do not be conformed to this world,*
> *but be transformed by the renewing of your mind.*
>
> Romans 12:2

3. Practice it before you preach it.

First we develop our faith; then we demonstrate it. Parents can't teach what they don't know, and they can't preach what they don't practice. Kids can spot a hypocrite at a thousand yards—blindfolded.

Be the first in your family to spend time with the Lord in the morning. There will be a day when your kids will stumble out of bed early, see you on your knees, and never forget it.

Be the first in your family to insist that Sunday was made for church. Go the extra mile and show them that the Sunday in the middle of your family vacation is also a day for the family to go to church together.

Be the first in your family to bow your head before you pick up your fork, at breakfast, lunch, and dinner—in private and in public.

4. Make family devotions a part of your life.

Just like many of you, my parents tried family devotions. Out came the overhead projector and the flannel board. Personally, I would have preferred a trip to the dentist for a root canal!

Devotions do not have to be painful, pointless, or prolonged. Ten minutes, two or three times a week, at the end of supper is plenty. On Monday, you may want to use Sunday's sermon or a Sunday school lesson as a starting point and then explore ways to apply the core concept to family life. On Wednesday, you could use a news item or current event to lead the family in a discussion about the question "What would Jesus do?" in this situation. Then on Friday, try using a Bible trivia game as a fun way to build faith. Also, if you're looking for ideas for making family devotions more fun and fruitful, I have found Jim Weidman's Heritage Builders series, a publication of Focus on the Family, to be very helpful.

5. Look for teachable moments.

Pray for teachable moments in the morning, look for them throughout the day, and experience them whenever they occur. Teachable moments happen during mealtime, drive time, playtime, bedtime, and all times in-between. They're captured, not created. They are "God opportunities" that may come in the form of a song on the radio, a beggar on the street, or an overpayment at the cash register. Each event provides an opportunity to teach how a scriptural principle, truth, or conviction is applied in a relevant manner.

Kids need to see faith in action. Through teachable moments, extend your kids' spiritual development by expanding their Sunday morning lesson into a weeklong experience.

It's like taking your kids from the classroom to the laboratory, from information to application.

6. Celebrate traditions.

Scripture is filled with examples of Jewish tradition. The Feast of the Passover, the Day of Atonement (Yom Kippur), and Hanukkah are just a few. Tradition gives us roots. It connects the present to the past. It defines our heritage—and it's not just for Jewish people.

Traditions can also serve to solidify our faith, so celebrate them or create them. Look back at a tradition that has been forgotten, or be creative and develop a new one. Look for unique ways to experience events like Thanksgiving, Christmas, and Easter. Possibilities include sharing personal experiences, reading a story, praying, or preparing and eating a special meal together. Then think creatively and develop traditions that celebrate birthdays, end of school years, and athletic achievements. In our home we honor family members by serving their supper on a special red plate. As kids grow older, these traditions will help keep your family connected—in a world that has many means of driving you apart.

P.S. It's closing time. The servers at Starbucks are dimming the lights and locking the doors. Our conversation has been warm, but our coffee has grown cold. Something tells us that it must be time to go.

We just want you to know that we consider it our privilege to have spent this time together. We prayed for you as we penned the pages of this book, and we will continue to pray for you as you apply these principles to your heart and home.

Parenting has no office hours and has a way of bringing the tough and the tender to their knees, but maybe that's the good news. It's on our knees that we come face-to-face with a God who turns the faint into the firm, the exhausted into the effective.

In no time at all, our kids will progress from diapers to driving. That's why we need to make today count by committing ourselves to the process of transforming totally average kids into totally awesome kids!

Teach your children to choose the right path,
and when they are older, they will remain upon it.
PROVERBS 22:6, NLT

Multnomah Publishers
The publisher and author would love to hear your comments about this book.
Please contact us at: www.multnomah.net/awesomekids

NOTES

INTRODUCTION

1. Sue Middleton, Karl Ashworth, and Ian Braithwaite, *Small Fortunes: Spending on Children, Childhood Poverty, and Parental Sacrifice* (Great Britain: Joseph Rowntree Foundation, 1997).
2. "Parental Priorities" *Infosearch: Current Thoughts and Trends Encyclopedia,* CD-ROM, version 4.2 (Arlington, Tex.: The Computer Assistant, 1998).

CHAPTER 2

1. D. Curran, *Traits of a Healthy Family* (San Francisco, Cal.: Harper and Row, 1983).

CHAPTER 3

1. Victor and Mildred Goertzel, "Cradles of Eminence," *Infosearch: Current Thoughts and Trends Encyclopedia,* CD-ROM, version 4.2 (Arlington, Tex.: The Computer Assistant, 1998).

CHAPTER 4

1. Dr. Samuel S. Janus and Cynthia Janus, *The Janus Report on Sexual Behavior* (New York: John Wiley and Sons, 1993), 169.
2. *Today in the Word* (August 1989), 21.

Chapter 5

1. Robert Schuller, *Self-Esteem: The New Reformation* (Waco, Tex.: Word, 1982), 18.
2. Karen S. Peterson, "Confidence Helps Foster Learning," *USA Today,* 24 October 1991, 1D.
3. Dale Wasserman, *The Man of La Mancha* (New York: Random House, 1966), as quoted in Schuller, *Self-Esteem: The New Reformation.*
4. Kevin Leman, *Bringing Up Kids without Tearing Them Down* (Nashville, Tenn.: Thomas Nelson, 1995).
5. This is a great book with specific examples to help parents build their child's self-worth. Jody J. Pawel, *The Parent's Toolshop: The Universal Blueprint for Building a Healthy Family* (Springboro, Ohio: Ambris Publishing, 2000).

Chapter 6

1. Charles C. Finn, "Please Hear What I'm Not Saying," © by Charles Finn. Used by permission of the author.
2. Lee Ezell, *Will the Real Me Please Stand Up?* (Nashville, Tenn.: Thomas Nelson, 1995), 154.
3. Margery Williams, *The Velveteen Rabbit* (New York: Simon & Schuster, 1983), 103–4.

Chapter 7

1. Roger Ekirch, "Why Johnny Can't Sleep," *Star-Telegram,* 18 November 2001, G1.
2. Lisa Whelchel, *Creative Correction: Extraordinary Ideas for Everyday Discipline* (Wheaton, Ill.: Tyndale, 2000).

Chapter 8

1. Amy Beth Graves, "Killer Desperate for Baby: A Chance Meeting in Store Doomed Pregnant Woman," *Star-Telegram,* 8 October 2000.
2. "Teen Arguing over Bike Killed in Ft. Worth," *Star-Telegram,* 30 December 2000.
3. "CDC's Reproductive Health Information Sources," *US Department of Health and Human Services,* 27 March 2002. http://www.cdc.gov/nccdphp/drh/surv_aport.htm (accessed 9 April 2002).

Chapter 9

1. Tom Harken, *The Millionaire's Secret* (Nashville, Tenn.: Thomas Nelson, 1998).
2. Lewis Carroll, *Alice's Adventures in Wonderland* (Cambridge, Mass.: Candlewick Press, 1999).
3. Nadine Stair, "If I Had My Life to Live All Over Again," taken from Leo Buscaglia, *Living, Loving & Learning* (New York: Holt, Rinehart and Winston, 1982), 122.
4. Todd Duncan, *The Power to Be Your Best* (Nashville, Tenn.: Word, 1999).
5. David Seel, *Parenting without Perfection* (Colorado Springs, Colo.: NavPress, 2000).
6. Paul Faulkner, *Raising Faithful Kids in a Fast-Paced World* (West Monroe, La.: Howard Publishing Co., 1995).
7. J. Canfield, M. V. Hansen, L. Hewitt, *The Power of Focus* (Deerfield Beach, Fla.: Health Communications Inc., 2000).

CHAPTER 10

1. George Barna, "Teens and Adults Have Little Chance of Accepting Christ as Their Savior," Barna Research Online, 15 November 1999. http://www.barna.org/cgi-bin/PagePressRelease.asp?PressReleaseID=37&Reference=B (accessed 9 April 2002).